A Creative Toolkit of Meditations

William Blake

BALBOA.
PRESS

A DIVISION OF HAY HOUSE

Balboa Press books may be ordered through booksellers or by contacting:
Balboa Press
A Division of Hay House
1663 Liberty Drive
Bloomington, IN 47403
www.balboapress.com
1-(877) 407-4847

Printed in the United States of America.

ISBN: 978-1-4525-7439-4 (sc)
ISBN: 978-1-4525-7441-7 (hc)
ISBN: 978-1-4525-7440-0 (e)

Library of Congress Control Number: 2013912151

Balboa Press rev. date: 10/04/2013

Acknowledgment

Several friends have helped me write and rewrite this book, bless them. I wish to acknowledge their time, energy, and wisdom.

Reina Roberts invented and refined (four times) the colors and shapes of the front and back covers. Reina teaches world ecology at the high school where my wife Haygo teaches chemistry and biology. The three of us are friends, and I heartily enjoy Reina's knowledge, humor, and art work. She's a winner.

Glenda Ryan and I have critiqued each other's stories and articles for five years. Glenda recently started submitting more stories and articles and has sold several. She read through this book twice, and it was like a top scale, thousand-dollar-a-cut barber fixing up a disheveled war veteran. From little flaws to bloated paragraphs that required rewriting, Glenda cleaned up the prose like a devoted mother washes up a small child after its adventures in a muddy back yard. Glenda writes and critiques superbly.

The third pastor ministering to *A Creative Toolkit of Meditations* is Haygo, my wife. She didn't want the name "Haygo" appearing in the book, so I call her "Sophie" throughout. One of Haygo's strong suits is her keen analysis. She takes apart and recombines chemicals, people, books, politicians, and cultures.

I love to talk with her. But when she's ready to speak with me about a critiqued chapter, I tell her "Wait a few seconds." Now I spend a preparatory minute or two slowly and deeply breathing in and out so that I'm more relaxed when her literary execution begins. This book is hers as much as mine.

Contents

Introduction

Practicing reverence for life we become
good, deep, and alive.
Albert Schweitzer

According to numerous scientific studies, steady meditation encourages a healthier, longer, and happier life. I recommend that you watch the TV documentary The New Medicine, which details how meditation reduces stress and improves health and happiness. This book's content echoes the scientific truths presented in The New Medicine. Even the industrial and medical worlds are now beginning to deliver meditation practices.

I call emotional maturing *growing up*. Meditation assists us to grow up. The second end product of meditation is enlightenment, which I term *waking up*. I borrow the phrases "growing up" and "waking up" from writer John Welman.

Growing up involves observation of how our negative beliefs determine our motivations, and thus our actions. A powerfully analytical engineer can produce high-quality design products yet fail to listen and inquire when a colleague is explaining a project. His analytic monologue kills any true dialogue. It's painful for the monologuing engineer to observe and change his long-term belief, which he might discover is *I'm the best, so they must listen to me*, a belief itself derived from *I'm weak so I must impress others*. Once this engineer recognizes this restrictive belief, he can observe and feel his resistance to an attitude change. Then he can listen more carefully to others.

Those of us who learn to reflect on our beliefs not only observe them but also take action to correct them. This process can be interesting, stimulating, and often enjoyable.

However, we all have fears about this growing-up process of observing and assuming responsibility for our limiting beliefs. We're fearful that our emotional identities will evaporate. A man's strong identity as *father of this household*, although it infuses him with a sense of power and leadership, can limit his freedom to become a friendly equal with his wife and children. *Father of this household* is his basic strong suit. Realizing the origins and consequences of such belief-driven identities can weaken them and enable us to feel compassion for ourselves and others.

Waking up, life's second journey, is rarer. Not many people wake up to their true nature—the answer to the worldwide meditative question of *What am I?* This answer eludes us with its simplicity. Specific meditations of chapter 4 can achieve this breakthrough.

Our two life journeys, *growing up* and *waking up*, are distinct, usually sequential, yet interconnected. *A Creative Toolkit of Meditations* describes both journeys and provides meditations for each. However, we must proceed with steady dedication. Daily practice is essential. Meditating four hours a day for one week is shortchanging ourselves compared to twenty minutes a day for a month.

My ballroom dance teacher once told me, "Ten minutes' practice every day!" A dance teacher or workout trainer wants us to develop muscle memory. The same advice applies to meditation. We can slowly build the muscle of awareness. I've observed that a slow, steady format works well in my meditation classes.

To achieve awareness muscle, we can reset our emotions through meditative inquiry creating mental silence that serves up fresh answers guiding us to useful behavior. Every meditation I've ever studied promotes an inner peace and silence. As a result, we live inside this harmonious silence, this *here-and-now presence*.

You might be wondering why anyone requires a toolkit of meditations. Why aren't one or two meditations sufficient? For a few people, one or two are enough. Yet attendees in my classes have distinct preferences for particular meditations— and they often move on to others. Some like meditations that focus on inquiry into a personal issue such as, *How can I change my thinking so that my job is more enjoyable?* Other participants hold fast to meditations emphasizing mindfulness, a peaceful, unbiased observation of self and others. A good toolkit gives us choices that we can utilize and amend in the future.

Chapter 8 lists eight topics covered by this book's meditations and pinpoints which of the twenty meditations best dip into each topic:

1. Awareness of surroundings
2. Recognizing and experiencing our True Self as Consciousness/Energy
3. Effectively communicating with others
4. Connecting mind and body, relaxing
5. Probing into our deep-seated, childhood-based negative beliefs
6. Distinguishing between imperfections and weaknesses; minimizing reactive emotions by increased patience, courage, and being at ease

7. Releasing anger
8. Improving relationships

Readers can select specific meditations by scrutinizing chapter 8's list of these eight topics.

Meditation is not belief-based like traditional religion. It's a personal, scientific *inspection* and *experiment*, an experiential routine to discover what changes occur. And, as different scientists experiment with different procedures and observe different results, meditators can create their own meditative regimens. For example, we can stress either one, or both, of the two meditative styles, mindfulness and inquiry. If we're bombarded by a relationship problem, we can inquire into its origins and resolutions. If we want to focus on being more present and joyful, we'll take up mindfulness meditations.

A Creative Toolkit of Meditations is designed to help you develop your own meditative practice. In addition, we can profit from meditating with a partner, friend, or group.

You can dance all these major steps of the spiritual mission. This book's thesis thus becomes, *Create your own meditation and spiritual routines. Grow up and wake up.*

My life has been bouncy, up and down. A few years ago, I stopped bouncing at the *up* position and have rested in that happy place ever since. I wrote this book to help readers more quickly work their way up.

My life features five evolutionary stages. The first was the shallow Silent Generation mentality for those born between 1929 and 1945. We were taught to study hard, work hard, be successful, conform to social standards, and never reveal our deeper emotions—be strong with our outside world and dismiss our inner world. That's how my parents and their friends lived. That's how I lived for decades. This *outer* viewpoint resulted in exciting work teaching English for thirty-five years at a community college, good health, and adequate social connections. My failure to grasp a pulsating *inner* viewpoint resulted in poor relationships with soon-abandoned women and inadequate relations with my two children, who thankfully are functioning well in their current lives.

Deeply held beliefs can push us to excel but create limitations that prevent us from a more fulfilling life. Landmark Education calls such worthy but limiting beliefs "strong suits." My strong suit was *worldly success with restricted emotions.*

The second major phase of my life was my training at Kankakee Community College in Illinois. Kankakee instructed its teachers to deliver *learner-centered, experiential* classes, including weekly and monthly performance objectives. I also learned the facilitator's trick of siding with speakers and then asking probing questions that enlarged their perspectives.

Following two years at Kankakee, I taught thirty-five superb years at Santa Ana College in Southern California. During my last twenty years, over one hundred students published in quality journals and magazines. Despite exhaustive time critiquing papers, I loved this job.

My third phase of life started when I was about forty years old. Something was still missing. What was it? An incompleteness kept whispering, *You're not fully alive, Bill.* At this time, I tried out several spiritual technologies, including Rinzai Zen Buddhism, Dogzen awareness of awareness meditation, Vipassana Insight Dialogue, Eugene Gendlin's Focusing, Marshall Rosenberg's Non-Violent Communications, Katie Byron's The Work, and Ramana Maharshi's "I-I" inquiry contemplation. I spent a year or two seriously practicing each tool. I felt better, became happier, and enjoyed these practices. Yet I continued my up-

and-down emotional drama. *Why?* Why didn't one, or all, of these practices ground me in emotional peace?

Basically, I didn't recognize that my failure to spiritually awaken, to live fully, was caused by my incessant striving for perfection. I had become an addict for *insights* that lifted me up for a week or a month, but then allowed me to fall to the bottom of my emotional up-down pattern. The higher I was lifted, the further I fell. This *neediness for perfection* is one of the greatest dangers of self-exploration. I'm an exemplum for this long-term, troublesome striving, this belief-driven addiction to achieving insights. *Striving equals not arriving.*

The fourth phase began about fifteen years ago. No more conferences, workshops, or listening to gurus. Meditations became private, personal, and relevant to the daily issues I faced. I started looking at meditation as a friend willing to listen, help, guide, and encourage me to accept realities. Now calmer, I laughed at my struggling for perfection. I taught meditation classes and enjoyed them. Somehow, everything improved. I became lighter, looser, happier.

The fifth and last phase of my life was awakening to *What I Am.* This was a sudden recognition that brought on an hour of insights flooding my mind. This enlightenment experience has been with me for a while now, along with its related insights. I live it out second by second. Chapter 4 describes this awakening.

As you can guess from this story, my main interest is developing and offering a spiritual practice that *shortens the time* to awakening to *What I am.*

If you're an *action* person, you might prefer to start with each chapter's meditation: Chapter 1's meditation, then 2's, then 3's, to the end of the book. Or you could pick out the meditations that most address your needs, do them, and read the explanations afterward. For example, if you're having communication problems in an important relationship, chapter 5's meditation on investigative dialogue would serve you well. If you're choked up with the desire to find out what the sages mean by awakening or enlightenment, begin with chapter 4. In other words, choose whatever content, chapter, or meditation entices you. The table of contents is your guide to scouting out your preferences.

In contrast, if you're an *introspective* type, you're committed to understanding the *why* of everything. Therefore, you might prefer to successively read each chapter and then perform its meditations.

My toolkit of meditations is reader friendly in its presentation of a kit that can be utilized according to the reader's preferences. After all, each of us is quite distinct in our thinking. Learning to take care of ourselves—choosing what we want and don't want, and honoring that decision—is one core element of becoming authentically happy.

Section 1, *Growing Up,* the first three chapters, presents the core issues that we humans face moment by moment. A moderate amount of growing up information might be helpful before tackling section 2's *Waking Up* topic, enlightenment. Section 3, the integration of growing up and waking up, consists of chapter 5 (investigative dialogue), chapter 6 (relationships), chapter 7 (our stressful culture), and chapter 8's synopsis of the book plus four additional meditations.

Section 1

GROWING UP

Chapter One

WHAT IS CONSCIOUS AWARENESS?

> The problem of how to be mindful is actually resolved not through stressful effort but by relaxing, allowing, and observing what is already there.
> Rodney Smith, *Tricycle,* Winter 2011

Mesmerizing Focal Points Are Everywhere

After stepping into my complex's junior Olympic-length swimming pool, I shivered for a few seconds until pushing my head and torso below the water. I came up cold but refreshed. Then I swam my first lap and back, lay on the steps, and gazed ahead at the two eucalyptus trees outside the pool's fence. The left tree is tall and round. Hundreds of bright ash-green leaf clusters caught my attention. The sun's setting rays illuminated the cluster's complexity.

I thought, *Can the work of any artist compete with this incredible tree?*

What prompted me to bond with a tree and its leaves? For several years, my meditation practice had emphasized *attentive observation.*

We're captivated by physical beauty when great music or art frames our conscious awareness. An example of such framing was gifted to me during a South Rim Grand Canyon trip. Grand Canyon, earth's largest and most breathtaking crevice, has a visitor center called Watchtower designed by architect Marie Coulter in the 1930s. Watchtower, a circular tower with a winding staircase, takes visitors to four levels. On each level, dozens of Coulter-designed windows look out over the mile-deep canyon. Each offers unique focal points. Scores of brownish-red layers of rock stand unperturbed. A perfectly rounded granite cone thrusts up among piles of globular rocks. A cluster of mammoth, flat and smooth horizontal rocks abuts a canyon-deep vertical wall equally as flat and smooth as its neighboring rocks. Configurations of rocks and trees intertwine in oddly mesmerizing arrangements. These windows vacuum out intrusive thoughts, and thus we more directly perceive superlative Grand Canyon scenes. Becoming more mindful, we're shocked by their beauty.

Like Coulter's windows, some meditations provide frames or reminders of how to witness our surroundings. My appreciation of the exquisite details of my complex's swimming pool developed after several years of meditation grounding me in the recognition that my essence expresses itself as conscious awareness. Meditative practices, including this chapter's awareness of awareness, can propel us into more awareness.

During any particular experience, we can notice focal points. A focal point attracts us and vibrates for us. The tallness and roundness of the big tree was my first focal point observation. The second was the bright, ash-greenness of the leaf clusters. The third was the awesme complexity of the leaf clusters. These focal points did not detract from my overall awareness of the big tree itself. I saw the entire big tree and the entire little tree next to it. These trees were obviously outside the fence of the swimming pool. Yet my attention on the tree's three successive focal points emotionally and physically *connected* me to the tree and the entire environment. I became more alive. Each of these experiences was unique. In spiritual language, I was "present" or "here and now," "mindful." Most importantly, I was aware that I was consciously attentive, one after the other, to the tree's ovular form, then to the bright ash-greenness of the leaf clusters, then to the clusters' complexity, and then to the tree's location outside the fence. This form of awareness I call "conscious awareness" because we're self-aware of being aware of something.

My yoga teachers command students, "Be fully aware of each movement, posture, and breath." These teachers often use the term "mindfulness" for pure or conscious awareness of an activity and its focal points.

What keeps us disconnected from conscious awareness of our environment and its successive focal points? One answer is unconscious negative beliefs that continuously shoot out negative thoughts and feelings. I call these semiconscious negative thoughts and feelings *add-ons* because they're a nuisance added onto our otherwise happy lives. Chapter 2 provides extended definitions and examples of negative beliefs and their add-ons.

Last year at my church, a liberal, inclusive denomination, I taught forty minutes of this chapter's awareness of awareness meditation to a Coming of Age class for youngsters eleven to thirteen. I took twelve of them down the street until we reached an area with abundant trees and bushes. Then I guided them through the awareness of awareness meditation at the end of this chapter. When finished, we returned to their classroom, where I questioned them about their experiences. I began with, "When you were aware of being aware, did you see an object more clearly?" One boy's answer was, "I don't care about all those trees and flowers. I only care about cars. The cars did shine more when I knew I was looking at them. The colors especially." A girl responded with, "I felt a bit more . . . how do I say it? *There!* I was *there* with what you asked us to look at." A boy, who I later learned has a neurological disorder, reported, "I loved it. I *was* one tree. I *was* one house. But I couldn't do it for the two minutes you asked for. My mind kept screwing up with ideas." My reply to him was, "Great! If you do it only for one minute for each object, or only for ten or fifteen seconds, do that. Whatever works for you." He nodded with a smile. All the children spoke about their enjoyment of the meditation.

The following Sunday during the coffee break after the service, the Coming of Age teacher spoke with me. She shook her head in amazement. "The kids were excited after you left. They talked about the exercise the rest of the class. Only positives. No normal sneering at all."

I wondered, *What would these kids' lives be like if they took an awareness of awareness class during the entire last year of primary school?*

Base Awareness and Conscious Awareness

Working with awareness of awareness meditation, we recognize the distinction between *base awareness* and *conscious awareness*. When we're not present with objects and their focal points, we're in *base awareness* or on *automatic pilot*. We can drive a car for five minutes without being aware that we're actually driving. If we kiss our mate while on automatic pilot, our relationship has momentarily tanked. The kiss becomes merely a pleasurable sensation, like a quickly downed mouthful of beer. What is she for me? Just a physical kiss? Where is my affection, appreciation, and attraction for her?

Nevertheless, with base awareness we're somewhat attentive. Otherwise, no one would qualify for a driver license or a marriage certificate.

Why am I making a distinction between base awareness and conscious awareness? The answer is that the spiritual journey is about stabilizing our conscious awareness, our mindfulness. When we become mindful, trees shine with their contours and colors—their focal points. With pure, intentional, or conscious awareness, we knowingly connect with the outside world of objects and people, plus our interior world of thoughts and feelings. Doing so, we lose our emotional *attachment* that keeps us in base awareness. We're fully experiencing some reality, but we're free of any expectations about it, any judgments about it, or any fears about it. I expect my wife will arrive home by four o'clock. But I don't mentally fixate, or emotionally attach, to her arrival. Below is a summary of base and conscious awareness.

> Base awareness—the *automatic, involuntary, mechanical* operation of our five senses of seeing, hearing, smelling, tasting, and touching, plus what Buddhists call the "sixth sense" of thoughts and emotions.

> Conscious awareness—*intentional mindfulness* or *self-awareness* of the serial focal points of our experiencing. The more we're consciously aware of our inner and outer worlds, the more vibrant and enjoyable our experiences become.

Awareness in *The American Heritage Dictionary* has the synonyms of *cognizant, conscious, sensible, awake, alert, watchful, and vigilant. Conscious* is defined as, "Having an awareness of one's own environment and one's own existence, sensation, and thoughts," or, "Mentally perceptive or alert; awake . . . subjectively known or felt." My term "awareness of awareness" is matched by the dictionary's phrase "having an awareness of . . . one's own existence, sensation, and thoughts."

This distinction between being and not being *aware of our awareness* is so subtle that it escapes us almost the entire day. An urge to develop awareness of awareness is what keeps monks in isolated forest retreats for years. I'm certain that this capacity for awareness can be best fulfilled in an environment of ordinary work and relationships.

Is Conscious Awareness Supposed to Make Us Happy?

People love mindfulness *when it pleases them*. Paradoxically, most people go into fear, anger, doubt, or disappointment when they become consciously aware of a distressing thought or emotion. As a single man, it wasn't important that I dressed for a party in black slacks and a mild brown shirt. After I began living with my wife, Sophie, she'd exclaim, "No! No!" at such clothing choices. I felt abused. Although I was grateful for her astute criticism of my colors and styles, I suffered when I became mindful that my outfits were aesthetically lacking.

I meditated on this abused sense and unearthed a negative belief from childhood: *trying to appear high-class attractive is not right because I'm not worthy of looking great.* I dressed cleanly, at least, but not elegantly. Now that I'm aware of my dressing motivation derived from this childhood-based belief, I dress much better. I also appreciate—rather than loathe—Sophie's advice about my dressing habits.

Mindfulness *includes conscious awareness of our suffering caused by negative beliefs.* Therefore, we can wrongly identify mindfulness as the *source* of our suffering rather than identifying our *attachment to negative beliefs* as the source of our suffering.

We devalue conscious awareness when we confuse our negative beliefs with their expression through conscious awareness. Regarding high-class dressing, *I'm not worthy* was my deeply seated, unconscious belief. *Appearing high-class attractive is not right* was this belief's add-on expression, which I initially considered an okay response. After I understood that this supposed *response* was actually a negative *reaction* to the belief *I am unworthy*, I let it go with, *It's totally all right to dress elegantly.* Sophie now appraises me as, "A lot more acceptable with your clothes."

In sum, mindfulness (even if uncomfortable) of a negative *reaction* can convert it into a positive *response.* If we comprehend this dynamic, mindfulness becomes 100 percent beneficial. Chapters 2 and 3 articulate negative beliefs, their reactive add-ons, and the path to terminating their harsh effects on us. The mantra is, *Be fully mindful of both negative reactions and positive responses.*

In spiritual literature, this period of conscious awareness causing emotional pain is called "dark night of the soul." Spiritual seekers (everyone is a seeker to some extent) must struggle through their dark night before arriving at awakening or enlightenment. After we blow through our uncomfortable dark night, *intuitive knowing* transforms us into more secure, friendly people. The seeker must realize that her dark night is not permanent. *It's an essential and temporary phase of the self-growth journey.*

Identical discomfort occurs with physical training. What if our body is aching and our gym coach commands us, "Five more push-ups"? We can relax our bodies with the thought, *This is an okay ache. If I keep up this training, these aches will gradually disappear.* Likewise, mental-emotional aching caused by meditation diminishes if we steadily perform our selected meditations.

Where does the lower self (suffering due to negative beliefs) and the upper Self (mindfulness or conscious awareness) contend for the prize of domination? This brawl occurs inside *me*. I am the main character of this incredible theatrical production, just as you're the main character of your drama. We (the main characters with all their misbehaviors) can solicit mindfulness to release and finally laugh at stifling beliefs controlling us. This same drama of ego versus conscious awareness occurs in all human lives.

At the summit of the spiritual journey, mindfulness takes over. Our self, our sense of separation or conditioning transmitted by our parents and culture, largely vanishes. Now mindfulness, or S̲elf, vibrates with its inherent bliss, wonder, and silence.

Meditation on Awareness of Awareness

Carry out the details of this meditation according to your intuition. After mastering this meditation, you more fully will recognize your capacity to choose and to connect with worldly objects. You'll respect your own *awareness of your awareness* as the king and queen of your life's parade of experiences.

Awareness of awareness meditation can be practiced any time during your waking hours. This active-time (i.e., anytime) meditation will increase your mindfulness of external objects. The instructions for this meditation appear complex, but after you do it a few times, they become quite simple.

Because it trains the mind, this is a mindfulness meditation.

At least fifteen minutes a day is recommended, but add minutes if your time restraints allow.

Several students from my classes practice awareness of awareness more diligently than any other meditation they learned. One in particular, Ruth, mastered utilizing it whenever she had a distracting thought. Ruth told the group, "When I think something negative, I look around and pick out a pretty setting. I focus on one or two focal points and quickly carry out awareness of awareness. Maybe it takes a few seconds or a half minute. Then I'm back to being present. At night, I do a longer version of it."

Instructions

For this meditation, select any environment that appeals to you. It could be a corner of your backyard, your work desk, bedroom window looking out at trees and clouds, or a kitchen cabinet topped with items.

First be consciously aware of one central item of this setting. Second, be aware, one after another, of the eight focal points of this one object:

> one through five: the five senses: sight, taste, sound,
>   smell, touch
> six: luminosity (degree of brightness)
> seven: space around it
> eight: space between it and you

Perhaps you choose the right kitchen counter as your meditation setting. Select objects on this right counter. Your first object might be a banana. Observe *one* banana's features (sight), peel it to hear it, taste it, smell the banana, and touch it. Next, observe the space between it and other objects on the counter. Finally, notice the distance between it and you. For each of these eight focal-point assessments, *make sure that you're aware of your awareness of each focal point.* Other terms for *awareness of awareness are conscious awareness and mindfulness.*

Next shift to a second object on the counter, perhaps a bottle of wine. Once more, play with the eight focal points of this bottle. *Be aware of your awareness* of each focal-point sensory experience.

For this meditation, you might choose one setting and then two or three objects, or focus on one object. Don't be rigid about observing all eight focal points for each object. Meditation is all about enjoying your experiences.

Chewing Meditation

Below is the simplified paraphrase of "chewing meditation/ chew this over" from *Awakening the Buddha Within,* a bestselling book by Lama Durya Das. Most of the commentary and the italicized sentences are mine. It's a classic Buddhist meditation.

This meditation specializes in mindfulness. Like conscious breathing, chewing meditation makes our perceptions more vivid and satisfying. Its focal points are clear and pulsating.

Chewing meditation can be expanded to include all foods and activities. Several participants in my meditation classes have substantially dropped weight after spending a couple of months real-timing this meditation. They eat slower and, hence, less food.

Two minutes for each raisin might be sufficient for you.

1. Sit down and relax. Put three raisins in your right hand. One is for your spiritual community. One is for your spiritual guide. One is for your spiritual path. Play with these three raisins. Examine them closely. Feel them as if you've never seen one before.

2. With your left hand, pick up one raisin. Study its colors and shapes. Feel its surface. Smell it. Especially, be aware of any opinions about your associations with raisins and their taste. Do you usually gobble raisins? Throw them over your dish of fruits?

3. Place it in your mouth and chew it as slowly as possible. Don't swallow it. Just softly and lovingly chew it. Mindfulness is all about *attention*, so pay attention to your thoughts, such as, *Wow! I've never tasted a raisin before. This is a ridiculous meditation. It's delicious—I want to swallow it now.*

4. When you have a thought unrelated to this meditation, notice if you're harsh with ourself: *I got all these thoughts! I can't even pay attention to eating a raisin.* Then return to simply examining this raisin.

5. Chew the raisin dozens of times while experiencing every aspect of it, as if it were the final event of your life.

6. Swallow the raisin and examine a second one just like you did the first. Put it into your mouth with your left hand. Once again, fully experience every facet of its existence. It's your lover, your entry into heaven. Finally, repeat these actions with the third raisin.

Chapter Summary

What do we see when we look at our desk cluttered with objects? Right now, I see the whole bloody mess. Yet if I note what attracts my vision, I'll discover that *each glance at my mess is most acutely focused on one object.* Right now, even though I see the entire mess, my eyes most prominently identify a *black and white pen.* Now I go back to typing, and immediately the *line of words* I just typed take charge of perception, even though I witness the whole page. Suddenly, my vision grabs onto the last word I typed, the last sentence's word with its period, *"page."* I lean back a moment and again notice the desk's clutter, but now the central object is the roundness of the lenses of a *pair of glasses* to the right of the black and white pen. I breathe deeply, and sense the *pleasurable expansion in my whole upper torso.* All in all, five focal points are experienced within four to five seconds:

- the *blackness and whiteness* of a pen
- a *line* made up of words
- the word *typing* with its *period*
- the *roundness of two lenses in a pair of glasses*
- the *pleasure* and *expansion* of my chest on an in-breath

Each of these central objects getting the most attention—one by one all day long—I call focal points. Anything can be a focal point, including a thought in our minds. Eight physical perceptions (modes of experiencing) produce focal points. We perceive focal points with sight, sound, touch, taste, and smell, plus luminosity, space around the focal point, and space between the focal point and us. The last three are also sight perceptions.

No one can 100 percent consciously identify all the focal points around her all day long. Yet we can fully experience and enjoy any focal point, for example the enticing smell of a steak being barbecued, and follow up with a grateful thought: *Ummmmm. Smells good!* Of course, negative thoughts ripping into us are also focal points (e.g., the guilt when we think, *Why did I miss that doctor's appointment?*).

When we experience anything, we're in one of two states. Either we're *aware that we're aware* of what we're experiencing, or we're on *automatic pilot*, probably functioning well but without full self-awareness of what we're experiencing. The first state we can call *mindfulness, attentiveness, conscious awareness*, or *higher mind*. The second state I term *automatic pilot, base awareness*, or *lower mind*. The purpose of meditation is to develop more and more mindfulness and increasingly bypass base awareness, including negative thoughts.

Chapter Two

BELIEF SYSTEMS AND THEIR ADD-ONS

Finite to fail, but infinite to venture
Emily Dickenson

Mindfulness Can Overcome Add-ons

Negative beliefs flail us. The first flails were designed in the Middle Ages to thresh grains such as oats. After one or two spiked metal balls were attached with chains, they became devices for torture. Our negative beliefs flail us with hurtful add-ons.

Add-on is a simple term that can assist our understanding of the mechanics of unhappiness. The "add-on" is the *extension* of an unconscious belief. For example, *I need to be married to be happy* is an extension of the belief *I am unworthy*.

Below are examples of the distinctions between a reasonable assessment of a situation, a core negative belief about it, and an add-on (extension) to that belief.

Reasonable Assessment	Core Belief Flailing Us	Add-ons
I'm a steady, heavy drinker.	Something's wrong with me.	A few drinks are good for me.
I'm late for this party.	I can do whatever I want!	The hell with this party!
This is a tough diet.	I don't have strong will-power.	A small slice of pie is enough.
This draft is a good rough draft.	I'm not creative.	No reader will enjoy this draft.
Regular workouts are important for my health.	I'm nothing without my buddies around.	I'll skip tonight's workout to beer up with the guys.

The trick of growing up is to become consciously aware of our belief-based add-ons. If we're observant of our add-ons, we can defeat them. That's one purpose of this chapter's meditations and of Chapter Three's OFRA practice which instructs us to Observe, fully Feel, take Responsibility for, and take Action to release our add-ons.

I'm unworthy generated thirty-five years of soul searching during which I deeply practiced six spiritual traditions. Each helped a little, but none worked profoundly until I seized upon a heart-centered practice fifteen years ago. I won't describe it because each of us must discover what practice works best for him or her.

Unconscious belief systems drag down conscious awareness, which attentively observes our outside world of work, canyons, and mates with all their intricacies. Conscious awareness or mindfulness observes both our outside and inside worlds. Through viewing *both* landscapes, we can disable the lower self's hostility toward mindfulness.

We customarily consider the lower self (misguiding negative beliefs with their constant add-ons) a "default" or basic, steady state. I guarantee that ol' ego *energetically* fights to stay active by shuttling us down its path of hidden beliefs whose add-ons entangle us. If we're passive, we consent to add-ons. We must audacious train ourselves to be mindful (consciously aware). The meditations of the first three chapters are tools for such training.

A synonym for conscious awareness is "mindfulness." With mindfulness, add-ons are harmless empty thoughts. Below are several upward shifts from automatic pilot awareness to mindfulness:

- Greater observation of our inner worlds of thoughts and feelings.
- Surging physical pleasure due to lessened stress and reactivity.
- A more liquid, rapid flow of energy that bumps up performance in all areas of life, including work, relationships, and physical activities.
- Diminished addictiveness, including over-shopping, over-eating, and alcoholism.
- A greater feeling of safety due to our enhanced self-confidence.
- *Stronger* negative emotions, including anger, confusion, loneliness, sadness, but with a much faster *acceptance* of these emotions, and thus a separation and emotional distance from them (i.e., non-attachment).

These beneficial changes are related to actual changes in our brains. All in all, we might consider mindfulness the most critical education or training of our lives. Yet this aspect of intelligence can remain a dream. Ego, our conditioning from infancy, can edge out mindfulness. In Chapter Five, I'll describe how Sophie and I deliberately, and often comically, communicate our own and each other's add-ons in order to grow our happiness garden. Genuinely happy couples are skilled at derailing their own and their mate's add-ons. They dexterously switch an add-on into a potential positive response.

A Brief Look at the Science of Meditation

All meditations in this book reduce stress. Stress is a physical symptom of impending danger. When we sense something dangerous might happen, the cerebral cortex shoots an alarm signal to the hypothalamus which releases the hormones adrenaline and cortisol into the bloodstream. Now the fight-or-fight response (sympathetic nervous system) peaks to lower the threat to our system. Blood pressure, respiration rate, and heart rate dial up. Blood shifts away from our extremities and guts into our brain and muscles, which tighten for fighting or running away. At this point, all of our sense organs operate at maximum efficiency: hearing, seeing, feeling, taste, smell. Like dopers, we're high.

So far, so good. But what happens to dopers? Too much dope reverses the high to an exhausted low. Likewise, if anyone is over-exposed to stress, to adrenaline and cortisol, the hormonal high fades into exhaustion. We have trouble concentrating, sleeping, and remembering. Three brain hormones help us balance the amount of adrenaline and cortisol that create energy but also, when over-produced, create stress. Serotonin gives us sound sleep. The second hormone, noradrenaline, governs our daily cycle of energy. If stress brings it down, we're flat exhausted. The third hormone, dopamine, produces happiness, enjoyment, and harmony with daily experience. With a lot of stress, and thus less dopamine, we slip into fatigue and exhaustion. In addition, dopamine relates to the release of endorphins from the brain. Endorphins, which are associated with opiates including morphine and heroine, slow down pain. In short, the sympathetic system producing adrenaline and cortisol enables a higher flow of energy; they cooperate with the hormones serotonin, noradrenaline, and dopamine, which respectively provide sleep, a proper cycling of energy throughout the day, and enjoyment.

The purpose of the *growing up* journey is to reduce add-on stress so that mindfulness triumphs. As noted from the paragraph above, such stress reduction has a bodily, physical, and hormonal component. Training the body-mind is intrinsic to meditation. Perhaps that's why hospitals, athletes, and even the military are now becoming involved in meditative practice. It's more than esoteric and mystical. It's cost-effective. It's practical.

The Long Range Impact of Childhood Beliefs

In an article entitled *What Ails Us* in the August 2012 The Sun magazine, Dr. Gabor Mate writes that "nearly 50 percent of American adults have a chronic illness." One major cause, says Dr. Mate, is that "The human brain develops in interaction with the environment, and the first three years of life are the most critical." Children reflect their environment, and do so the rest of their lives. If children don't receive adequate *love* and *support*, they're stressed out.

What is nurturing parent behavior? Mate writes that we find much less chronic diseases like ADD in hunter-gatherer societies because of

> three qualities they provide in child rearing. Number one: small children are always in close, nurturing physical contact with adults. They're carried everywhere. They're rarely put down, and they're certainly not left without nurturing adults even for a moment . . . Number two: the child is cared for by a whole set of nurturing adults, not just one or two. There's a tremendous sense of safety and security in that. As the saying goes, it takes a village to raise a child. Number three: Hunter-gatherers don't believe that a five-month-old child should be independent enough to 'cry it out' and put himself to sleep. That kind of practice is encouraged only in so-called civilized societies. When children in a tribal society are distressed, they are immediately picked up and soothed, before their brain is overwhelmed by stress hormones during a critical period of its development. Stress releases cortisol, which interferes with the hippocampus, the memory center. And stress overwhelms the emotional centers of the brain. When children don't learn how to regulate their stress internally, they're prone to do it later through drugs or addictive behaviors, such as overeating.

I'll provide one last quote from Dr. Mate's profound article. "There are genetic predispositions to addictions, but they don't cause addiction by themselves; they just increase the risk. In both animal and human studies subjects don't become addicted if they receive proper nurturing, even in the presence of predisposing genes."

For months, our front door's grainy surface had fascinated me. Every day I spent at least an hour examining its dark brown surface with black lines embedded into thousands of small grooves. That afternoon, I ran my fingers over areas surrounding the silver knob, where the indented black threads lived beside the brown wood.

As I enjoyed the door's face, my four-year-old mind kept pondering the question occupying me for several weeks. *Why are Mommy and Daddy sad? Why is Mommy sad all the time? Her face is so sad. Daddy is sad when he comes home. He smiles at Little Brother Hay and me but doesn't smile when we eat dinner.*

With renewed interest I re-inspected the dark brown wood with its black gullies. Back and forth I travelled, from the curiosity of *Why are Mommy and Daddy sad?* to the sheer pleasure of my beloved front door. Suddenly an entirely new series of thoughts leapt into mind. *Gramma Muzzy doesn't make Mommy and Daddy sad. She cooks on Sunday. Mommy and Daddy like to eat her food . . . Little Hay doesn't make Mommy and Daddy sad. He can walk now. He's a good baby. Blue poops on the rug. But he doesn't make Mommy and Daddy sad. Everyone likes Blue. Blue is a good dog.*

No one else lived with us. No one else was making my parents unhappy. I re-examined the front door, my aesthetic treasure.

Two or three minutes skated by before the answer popped into mind.

I make Mommy and Daddy sad. Not Gramma Muzzy. Not Little Hay. Not Blue. I make them sad.

I was relieved. My quest was over. The belief that I, Billie, was the cause of my parents' sadness solved my quandary. Contented, I re-studied the front door's wood.

Within a minute, three beliefs surfaced in succession.

I have to stop making Mommy and Daddy sad. I'm bad because I make Mommy and Daddy sad. I have to be better.

That belief, *I am unworthy*, now ingrained into my nervous system at age four, was to shape a future of less-than-happy relationships with women: The formula is *I am unworthy ———>I make Mommy sad ———>I have to be better ———>I have to help my woman fix herself.* Because all my ladies (my Mommy) supposedly were infected with emotional flu, I had to help them fix their flu. *Ouch!* was the result for the women I lived with.

I am unworthy cultivated *I don't like myself* which sponsored a pervasive, subtle attitude of *I don't really like and enjoy others.* Everyone has some variation on the belief *I am unworthy.*

> *I can't be a leader. I'm a follower and can't get into truly creative work.*
>
> *I have to be the best (dutiful, rich, admired, super-attractive, smartest).*
>
> *I just have to get by. That's all I can do.*
>
> *Life is too difficult to really enjoy.*
>
> *I don't really like and enjoy women (or men).*
>
> *Others are stupid . . . I don't have to be loving toward them.*
>
> *I'm better and smarter than others.*

The last two beliefs on this list appear to be the opposite of *I'm unworthy*, but they're adaptive reactions, or overlays to, *I'm unworthy.* Many real-life miseries result from *Others are stupid . . . I don't have to be loving toward them* and *I'm better and smarter than others.*

Before Awakening, the Dilemma of Two Selves

So, at age four I possessed two selves. A child from birth to three or four years old keeps bursting out with genuine love, vivacity, caring, and a generally peaceful mind. I loved helping Dad gather up the dishes for washing. I vivaciously scratched Blue's head and rolled around on the lawn with him. I cared about Mom when I carried a grocery bag to our car after Mom shopped. I treasured quiet and silence when resting after playing for hours. Before sleeping, I listened to the faint sounds of my parents talking in the living room. A child has many of the traits of the awake state. We witness their incredible spontaneity, joy, connectedness, eagerness, and even humor. Jesus was correct when he said, "Be like a child."

This book describes a process of adults slowly but steadily, through meditation, rediscovering this childhood true self of spontaneity, connection, and joy. We can move from a *conditioned self*, an ego, hounded by negative beliefs to a higher, more mature Self.

In brief, a one-year old child dances with his or her organic True Self. In contrast, by three-five years old, without the full security and freedom that excellent parenting provides, a child begins suffering from the *psychological conditioning* of ingrained fear, doubt, over-concern, anger, and/or sadness. At this juncture, *growing up* becomes necessary for greater happiness. The truth that *growing up* usually begins in middle age is a serious indictment of our culture.

By four years old, the majority of children are neurologically ingrained with negative beliefs about themselves and other people. Through adulthood, these onerous beliefs can be deepened or diminished by environmental influences.

We all have some degree of *both* a positive higher Self and a negative lower self. The trick is to evolve more and more into the positive higher Self by transforming lower-self negative energies into love for ourselves and others. However, when we attempt to *eliminate* the lower self, at that precise moment we're doomed to failure. The lower self is real, unavoidable, and in numerous circumstances supports us in daily activities.

The belief *I'm unworthy* is my "constructed self." It was constructed by my parents, larger family, culture, and myself. By the time we're five years old, our psychic constructions have settled into the synapses and dendrites of our brains. As adults, our work is to create a toolkit of friendships, activities, and meditations to foster *self-observation* that will illuminate negative conditioning. The science-based book *The Folly of Fools* by Robert Trivers cites examples of *I have to* reactions. It teaches us that our generic self-deceit leading to deception of others originates in the brain's medial prefrontal cortex. Neurological science, psychology, and meditation theory are now interfacing like the parts of a bicycle.

Through steady meditative practice, our lower, constructed self can be adroitly managed. We don't have to be like frogs in hot water, acclimatizing to hotter and hotter water until they stop breathing. In this analogy, the water is the cultural conditioning that afflicts almost everyone to some extent. I do have a few friends who seem to be mostly free of conditioning, bless them.

Our lower, conditioned self can be likened to a diseased plant which has some rotten roots (beliefs). Some of the budding leaves are toxic add-ons. Digging out this diseased plant's rotten roots isn't fun, but we're grateful when our healthy plant grows firm, tasty leaves.

Below is a schematic review of the *awake, growing up (higher) Self,* and *conditioned (lower self))* states. Our psychic states constitute a spectrum, and we all have at least a small piece of all three states. Identifying where we are prompts us to evolve.

AWAKE OR ENLIGHTENED STATE: Addictive beliefs and their add-ons are almost vanished. We feel ourselves unified with, and paradoxically distinct from, everything and everyone. A "thought" is real but its contents understood as illusory. Our zest to keep learning and to connect with everything and everyone is amplified. We have a lot of humor about our own flaws and those of others. We're cogent that all humans are equal. A sense of Oneness radiates within and through us. We recognize our essence, What I Am.

GROWING UP: *Higher mind functioning.* Conscious awareness promotes openness, increased mental and emotional spaciousness, and greater happiness with our work and social relationships. We desire and seek out activities that cause positive changes. Times can be tough and our conditioning from childhood is still active, but heavy tension is sporadic, not continuous. We're learning to appreciate and enjoy spewing out humorous comments about ourselves and others. Yet a subtle, background tension is moderately disturbing.

LOWER MIND CONDITIONING: Fear, boredom, guilt, doubt, sadness, *should be / should do* thinking, and a sense of separation significantly reduce mindfulness. We're basically unhappy and pretty much clueless why we're unhappy.

Most people move into a wide range of *growing up* that spreads out from minimal to radical self-examination. If people in this sector become involved in a sound meditative practice, they create the possibility of growing up more speedily and even discovering What They Are.

When we reach middle age, many of us re-consider what our core purpose is and realize that we're clueless about it. We think, *So far, I've basically done what the culture has told me to do. Is there a path that will make me more authentic, more happy?*

Good news! Even without a meditative path, research indicates that we become happier as we age. An article named "Wise Up" in the July-August 2012 *Smithsonian* magazine cites several studies that, even though "certain mental skills decline with age . . . scientists are finding the mind gets sharper at a number of vitally important abilities." According to a University of Illinois study, older air traffic controllers "excelled at their cognitively taxing jobs, despite some losses in short-term memory and visual spatial processing. How so? They were expert at navigating, juggling multiple aircraft simultaneously and avoiding collisions." In a 2010 study, University of Michigan researchers learned that "Dear Abby" letters of advice to 200 people written by people in their 60s "were better than younger ones at imagining different points of view, thinking of multiple resolutions and suggesting compromises."

Managing emotions is a critical skill, and elders do it better than youngsters. "In 2010, researchers at Stony Brook University analyzed a telephone survey of hundreds of thousands of Americans and found that people over 50 were happier overall, with anger declining steadily from the 20s through the 70s and stress falling off a cliff in the 50s." A similar finding occured with Laura Carstensen, a Stanford psychologist who "led a study that followed people ages 18 to 94 for a decade and found that they got happier and happier and their emotions bounced around less." The article's conclusion is that "Such studies reveal that negative emotions such as sadness, anger and fear become less pronounced than in our drama-filled younger years."

We don't need to wait decades. Let's skip ahead of this time-bus to happiness by cutting down our "negative emotions" right now.

An inspection of our egos is *difficult*. It's not an easy walk around our well-tended local park. The majority of my meditation participants experience uncomfortable sensations when first meditating. They protest that "Thoughts keep coming into my mind. I can't find any silence within my mind." My replies to participants include these:

> "It takes time to train the mind. Be patient. Don't be ordered around by your ego. When thoughts intrude, breathe them in and exhale them out with a friendly *Bye Bye*."

> "Great! You're on the spiritual journey. You're *observing* that your ego is climbing over the wall of your privacy to dump thought after thought into your mind. When you observe such thoughts, say to yourself something like, *I am not my monkey-mind thoughts*. Or simply think, *I am the awareness observing these monkey-mind thoughts*."

For necessary support, you can enlist a friend who might be interested in self-growth. Converse with him or her about the difficulties or triumphs that you're encountering. Maybe you can create a team of three or four others who want to clean off the lower mind's muck. My lady Sophie and I have been meditating together for four years, and our relationship has substantially evolved. My meditation classes have prompted me through emotional thickets as much as they've assisted participants.

One Man's Struggle with Add-Ons

Until I forced my buddy Harry to pierce into his unconscious belief of *I'm incomplete*, he acted out his add-ons with women, especially *I have to live with a perfect woman who complements me and makes me complete.* Harry nefariously left his women after living with them only four or five months. A single man of late middle age, his demeanor is soft, gentle, gracious, and accommodating. He carefully listens to what others say, especially women. Retired with a good income, Harry is in sound financial shape and wears quality clothing. To many middle-aged women, he's a keeper.

Harry recently travelled to Oregon to visit with a son and commenced still another maybe—I'll—stick—around relationship with a woman. He told me in one of our bi-weekly phone calls that he had told her, "Amy, we could be life partners, but I'm not certain. We need time together." Then he continued with "I'm not sure about her! She's lively, educated, sexy . . . I like being around her. But something's not there. It's like . . . well . . . she's too controlling. Too demanding about what we do. A bit brusque. I wind up wanting to get away. Bill, I'm not sure if I really want her."

In a call three weeks later, after he'd spent a half hour describing his current pick-up, Judy, a sexy woman like Amy but who was "too peaceful, too placid for me," I knew that I had to tell Harry the explicit truth about his relations with women. We were best friends, and he'd been honest about my flaws.

The next time we talked, I pointed out seven of his add-ons that I'd typed out. They were caused by Harry's negative belief of *I'm incomplete and weak*:

1) A neediness to connect with people, especially women.
2) Without this connection, especially with women, loneliness.
3) Fear of connection with women. Fear of losing your imagined independence.
4) Fear and hatred of your mother. Leaving women equals power and independence. In other words, your turn all women into your mother.
5) Mania for spiritual workshops and contact with gurus delivers emotional highs. You go from one to another ad infinitum, like you do with your lovers.
6) Blankness about the emotional pain your women suffer when you dump them.
7) No authentic capacity to ask for what you want and to say "No" to what you doesn't want.

Harry is correct in identifying some female foibles. His women are as much at fault as he is for being sucked into a live-in relationship. They haven't assessed him correctly or carefully dialogued with him about his prior affairs. They're needy for an apparently up-scale man and let themselves be victimized.

Harry's submerged belief is *I'm incomplete and weak*, which energizes the above seven add-ons. These attitudes or add-ons are not "passive" because they *actively* coerce Harry to behave in deplorable ways. When we begin to observe our add-ons, ol' ego ferociously, cleverly, and deceptively fights back against conscious awareness. We lose our capacity to perceive emotional focal points. I call ol' ego the Ultimate Opponent for good reasons.

How did Harry respond to my analysis of his relations with women? He said, "I'm *shocked! Incredible!*" He paused for at least a half minute before he stammered, "Bill, thanks. It sounds real to me."

"Good, Harry. From now on in our raps, I want you to report on your observations of what's really happening inside you. The gurus you see all say the same damn thing: 'Observe what's really there.' Isn't that the platform of their teachings?"

"Yes . . . yes, it *is*. I'm dumbfounded."

"I'll e-mail you this list of seven possibilities for change."

Dumbfounded? I suppose so. Harry's core belief of *I'm incomplete* and its seven add-ons mentioned had been blurred from his conscious awareness.

Harry does retain an intellectual honesty when confronted with fact-based observations. I'm pleased that since I spoke with him about his womanizing, Harry has increased his sensitivity about how his hidden beliefs provoke add-ons which demolish his relationships.

Three Meditations to Clean Up Stress From Add-Ons

I was irritated when my wife Sophie came home exhausted from her exposure to two hundred high school students (about 30% incompetent or disruptive) for seven-eight hours, and then faced two more hours devoted to test corrections or preparation for the next day's classes.

Formerly I had desired her attention when she arrived at home. Through the use of the three meditations presented below, I now experience no neediness for her when she requires time to unwind from her exhausting job. The stress-producing belief *I have to be a better person by helping others* has disappeared with her and all others. The downfall of this self-destructive belief left me *much more helpful with everyone.* Good-bye, dire neediness.

I'm indebted to Dr. Mark W. Muese, author of *Practicing Mindfulness: An Introduction to Meditation,* for the first two meditations of this chapter. Dr. Muese employs the term "unwholesome thoughts" for my "add-ons." The explanations, descriptions, and instructions are almost entirely my own language.

"Recent neurological research," writes Dr. Muese, "has shown that routine patterns of thought create a propensity for more wholesome thoughts; unwholesome thoughts predispose the mind to produce more unwholesome thoughts . . . Meditation practice shows us that we can choose which thoughts to entertain and which to observe and release."

1 Replacement

Replacement tackles add-ons by replacing them with positive thoughts. The documentary *Secrets* gained widespread acceptance because its thesis was *positive thoughts tend to hatch more positive thoughts.* When we observe an add-on (negative thought or emotion), we can replace it with a positive one. Sometimes a negative thought or emotion vanishes quickly, within fifteen seconds. If it goes away that quickly, it's a natural human thought or emotion. If it lasts more than fifteen seconds, I term it an add-on caused by long-held negative beliefs. Chapter Three discusses this time limit with greater detail.

Whenever you observe a negative belief or add-on, think of a positive *replacement* word or phrase for it. On a 3 X 5 card, write out the add-on plus the replacement. The examples below show you the sentence pattern to use. The negative thought is first. The replacement thought, or thoughts, is after the arrow.

Many meditators might prefer to forget about writing anything on a card, but writing out this meditation will fuse it into consciousness.

I suggest carrying out the above meditation for two days, the second meditation of this chapter for two days, and the third meditation for two days. The seventh day do the one you like best.

If you pick # 1 or # 2, practice it at least eight to ten times a day for a few weeks. This precise practice will dump some of your beliefs into more tolerable back seat noises. Now they're not driving the car.

1. *I feel beaten up by Byron.* ——> I'll tell him, "Too harsh a tone," and then walk away.
2. I'm *annoyed* and *disappointed* with Dad talking about my "financial ignorance?" ——> Wrong! I'm on top of my money, and saving quite a bit.
3. I'm *guilty* for not exercising enough. ——> I do an hour in the gym six days a week. Screw you, guilt.

2 Redirection

The second meditation skill is "redirection." Redirection relates to "diverting attention away from the unwholesome thought to something more beneficial." Three examples are below. In these examples, the add-ons are the initial statement. After the arrow, the redirection is stated.

1) The management of this complex is awful. ——> A short, cordial letter signed by five or six jacuzzi buddies will convince management to keep the pool warm.
2) I screwed up because I didn't understand the Bundy contract. ——>I'll spend twenty minutes each day, starting today, cataloguing his business's ifs, hows, wheres, and whens.
3) Damn it! No newspaper again at 6 am, the arrival time. ——>Maybe the carrier is having a car or other problem.

Record the negative thought and related emotion on a 3 X 5 card plus the word, phrase, or activity used to reduce its power.

You can electronically record your notes. Also, you can utilize Facebook and Twitter to discuss your exploratons with friends.

Do this short exercise eight to ten times a day for a few weeks.

My class performs all three meditations when we have our second two-hour session. Most participants prefer # 1, but a few really appreciate # 2. Many exclusively stick with #3, below.

3 Breath Meditation for Negative Thoughts and Feelings

Many meditations use breathing tactics. I created this simple meditation to pierce into negativity.

> Whenever you observe a negative thought or emotion, breathe it in with a slow, expansive opening of your chest area. Then slowly breathe it out into a hundred miles of earth beneath your feet. Perhaps this negative thought or emotion requires two or three in and out breaths.

> A more sophisticated and powerful version of the above meditation is to in-breathe in the same way, i.e., in-breathe the negative thought or emotion with a slow, wide opening of the chest area. On the out-breath, exhale slowly and deeply while thinking *I am the awareness observing you, negative thought.*

You can perform this simple tactic while standing in front of an angry policeman upset because your group is rap dancing on the street rather than walking quietly. You can employ it while someone is subtly putting down your gender, creed, or race. It increases your calmness and self-control regardless of any circumstance.

Chapter Summary

Why are we hounded, each to a different degree, by emotional stress?

Negative add-ons are "extensions" of often unconscious or semi-conscious negative beliefs. A core negative belief flails us with add-ons. The belief *I'm unworthy* causes add-ons such as *I can't get a department promotion* or hostility toward a neighbor because he cuts his front yard grass differently than we cut ours. An angry or guilty *Maybe he's a better grass cutter* can briefly flood our minds. Negative beliefs reduce our aesthetic enjoyment, but identifying and derailing them enhance pleasure and happiness.

Considerable modern scientific research indicates that we can reduce add-on stress with meditation. For this reason, meditation is increasingly utilized by corporations, medical facilities, and churches.

Belief systems become ingrained in our nervous system in childhood. Children in cultures with "close, nurturing physical contact with adults" are less likely to suffer from diseases like ADD.

We all possess two selves, the "lower" or "conditioned" self that stresses us and the "higher" or "true" self that creates relaxed joy.

These two selves manifest together as one of three states that people inhabit.

> lower mind conditioning (usually dysfunctional
>   people)
> growing up (the majority of us)

awake or enlightened (a minority and usually
associated with an advanced degree of growing
up).

No human being has ever completely grown up, even
enlightened sages.

This chapter's three meditations reduce add-ons and foster
mindfulness. They're simple to practice.

Chapter Three

GROWING UP WITH OFRA

> To act without clear understanding, to form habits
> without investigation, to follow a path all one's life
> without knowing where it really leads—such is the
> behavior of the multitude.
> Mencius (372?-389? BC)

Knocking Out Negative Beliefs with OFRA

This section concentrates on the four steps of OFRA. With OFRA's observation, feeling, responsibility, and action, we learn to fully experience, accept, and ultimately laugh at our formerly hidden negative beliefs.

Observation is the first base of OFRA. If we can't observe a thought, emotion, or behavior, we can't take effective action to slice and dice it. Ethics, morality, compassion, and joy originate with observation.

How do we observe?

- We first slow down, listen, and pay attention.

- We notice any queasiness and ask *Why am I queasy about [my brother visiting me for a weekend]?*
- After asking a question, we slip into our silent mind.
- After a period of silence, silence can provide an answer.
- We can take brief, concise notes about what the silence reveals.

With practice, we can finally *know* the expectations and desires that our parents and their culture cemented into our brain's dendrites since our birth.

Feeling is the second component of OFRA. If we can't feel it, we can't deal with it. Nevertheless, experiencing fully can be painful. Negative thoughts and feelings are natural for everyone *for a short time*. Elizabeth Kübler-Ross, a well-regarded writer on sorrow and grief, wrote, "Anger is a natural human emotion; it lasts only fifteen seconds." What! Only "fifteen seconds"? Yes, Kübler-Ross is correct. Beyond fifteen seconds, we're idolizing our judgments and fantasies. After experiencing a negative thought-feeling for only fifteen seconds, we can return to now, even if that now is trimming a tree on a hot afternoon. Beyond fifteen seconds, we're faced with an add-on to a negative belief.

Full feeling and responsibility lead to appropriate action. Responsibility requires clarity regarding our self-proclaimed objectives. Every nutritionist advises his clients to keep a log of their food diary and exercise, and Weight Watchers give clients the right to use accumulated points at the end of the week. If a client ate seventeen of twenty points on Friday and fifteen of twenty on Saturday, he has the right to eat eight more points on Sunday.

Eating well, exercising steadily, finding a better job, being more supportive of our mate and children, and telling a good joke once a day are objectives that can slip back into oblivion due to our hectic lifestyle. Moreover, ol' ego, our lower self, hates our participation in happiness-producing activities, including meditation.

Action is the logical, appropriate result of observation, feeling, and taking responsibility, As we train ourselves in OFRA, its four components blend together. Observation triggers feeling, which initiates responsibility causing action. Living becomes a more cogent, fluid, happier unification of our experiences.

A principle for mastering OFRA is Go slow, small, and steady. As I stated in the Introduction, we can slowly, piece by piece, build "awareness muscle."

If I had to present a single sentence summarizing all the complexities and approaches of OFRA, it would be "Pleasurably *know* rather than defensively *believe*." We must observe, feel, take responsibility, and create action that reduces the energy of our add-ons. At that juncture, *intuitive knowing* will guide us rather than our belief-driven expectations and desires.

Consistent practice of OFRA, or something similar, encourages us to evolve from *thinkers* into *knowers*. *Knowers* inhabit a spacious mansion with windows and doors open for fresh breezes. Self-aware *knowing* is an intuitive assessment of each distinct context, moment by moment.

Knowing, the product of critical thinking based upon OFRA, wins out over *commonplace thinking* because it's been developed through self-observation of add-ons. A good ninth-grade teacher will precisely observe and intuitively respond to a child's "You're stupid, teacher!" remark. The teacher *knows* that this student's identity centers around abuse of authority. With this clarity, the teacher projects no anger or disappointment toward this young boy. Instead, she responds with a gracious, "Thank you!" or shake of her head before saying, "Put your head down on your desk and help our class by saying nothing the rest of the period." Or she smiles at the boy and says, "Time for you to go to the office. I'll be sure to give your parents a call tonight." This teacher's affable response also lays out firm consequences for behavior that threatens classroom protocol and respect for instructors.

OFRA Examination of Our Belief Systems

We live at a multifaceted spectrum of awareness, but two viewpoints predominate. One viewpoint is from the *conditioned* self that ranges from bewilderment to moderate happiness. The richer, higher self involves a journey of understanding this underlying, conditioned sadness and unhappiness. This is the *growing up* state.

Growing up expands our inner spaciousness. Our interior world takes in everything with more gusto, like a cat scrutinizing its surroundings, which it instinctively owns. We speak more freely. We see tough circumstances as negotiable. Although negative conditioning from childhood still engulfs us at times, we've gained some power over it. Expanded conscious awareness breathes positive energy into our minds and hearts.

Recognizing different stages of growth helps us navigate the hierarchy to more expansive happiness, like a karate student advances from a white belt (conditioned and unhappily challenged) to a brown belt (more confident and often happy) and then to a black belt (joyous and spiritually *awake*).

To shift more and more out of unhappy conditioning into happy freedom, we must train ourselves in *critical thinking*, which in this chapter includes the four steps of OFRA.

Critical thinking involves actions and decisions based upon intelligent values such as healthy food choices: organic fish, fruits, vegetables, and gluten-free oatmeal rather than large amounts of sugar and processed foods. Attacking such critical thinking, the conditioned mind looks around the market and screams, *Those doughnuts look good! And . . . hhhh-nnnn-mmmm, doughnuts! Maybe I'll have only half a doughnut.*

What occurs when we tackle a hurtful pattern, for example ignoring a girlfriend's birthday? We commence with observation of our inaction. Next, we feel a *healthy* guilt about it. Third, we take responsibility by scribbling birthdays into our calendar. Fourth, we take action by arranging a party for her next birthday and discussing the details with her.

The following anecdote reveals how conscious awareness expresses itself as critical thinking and appropriate action. Two months ago, I was at a post office, and as I walked out the door I spotted a couple, Eddie and Jossie, I've known for years. We decided to eat lunch at a nearby restaurant. As we sat down, Eddie began his customary complaint about his oldest son, Aaron, who continuously criticizes him. According to Aaron's pronouncements, Eddie has failed as a father, the sole reason why this twenty-five-year-old son has failed to find work, construct a career, earn money, locate a woman, or create his own living accommodations. As I sat across from both of them, Eddie continued ranting about Aaron for at least a half hour. Once I interrupted him by asking Jossie a personal question. Twice she asked me personal questions that I answered, yet as soon as we'd made brief replies, Eddie would return to fulminating against Aaron. When Eddie wasn't noticing, Jossie glanced at me with a *How do I put up with this man?* look on her face.

During a half hour of listening to Eddie roar about his son, I formulated a plan. I finally interrupted him with, "Eddie, you're *not* in present time! You're operating from past-time expectations about what Aaron should do that you project into future time. You're not *here and now* with Aaron, or with us right now. You're *not present*, so you can't think critically."

Pausing, he glanced upward at the ceiling, shifted around in his chair, and stared at me. "I'm here. I'm talking about what bothers me. My son's behavior bothers me."

"What can you *do* when he goes into a verbal attack? What *action* can you *do* rather than harangue him about his failings?"

He paused again. Jossie said, "Bill's right. You've been living in the past for years. Aaron gets worse when you two talk against each other."

Eddie nodded slightly, opened his mouth to speak, and then said, "So . . . what do I *do*?"

"*Simple*. Too simple for a bright guy like you to figure out. Eddie, you believe Aaron needs your advice to change his behavior. You're such an intellectual guy that you believe language can change people. It worked brilliantly for you for thirty-five years running an international business, but it's diddly-do with Aaron. So . . . you tell him only once, in a simple sentence, that when he gets verbally offensive you'll raise up your right hand like this." I pushed my open palm forward and up. Eddie shook his head.

"That doesn't mean anything. He'll still continue bashing me."

"Then you walk away. You go into another room and read a book or watch television. First, signal with an arm raised that he must stop his rant. Second, leave if he continues treating you with disrespect."

"Interesting!" Jossie stared at me like I was some kind of ghost.

This *physical action* solved Eddie's problem with Aaron. They've stopped verbally blasting each other. I've described this physical-action approach to several other persons who wholeheartedly adopted it. Now they bypass arguments. They express what they want and don't want and, if necessary, perform a physical action, perhaps leaving, to seal in their desire.

Beliefs obliterate critical thinking. Eddie *believed* his parental job was to convert Aaron into a responsible and courteous son. He had a belief that *Words are the only real avenue of changing people.* Eddie's belief propagated endless add-ons when Aaron refused to listen and exploded with his own add-ons. Eddie had to examine his 100 percent belief in verbal solutions.

Like Eddie, believers with a lower viewpoint live in a small hut with convictions jamming the doors, windows, and chimneys. Not much moves in and out. It's a tight, dense milieu of *shoulds/should nots, expectations,* and *desires.* Our self-examination, our critical thinking, is limited.

Our thoughts often express our anxiousness (e.g., *Mom's questions about my dating drive me bananas. Mom wants to know every single detail.).* This young woman can utilize OFRA critical thinking with her mother. She first closely *observes* her mother's compulsion to be told every whippet of last night's date. She *feels* Mom's fretting about her dating. Next, this young lady assumes *responsibility* to figure out *why* Mom is so demanding about this issue. She takes *action* by sitting down and asking herself, *Why is Mom so concerned with my dating men?* She allows her mind to become silent and thus divulge an answer. After a session or two, the silence can dish out something like, *Well . . . she dated and married Father. She doesn't want me to get trapped in his narrow views about what a woman can do and not do. She's living out her own dilemma.* With such an understanding, this daughter now has compassion for her mother. Even more, she *knows* her mother well enough to ask questions and make comments assisting her mother to observe her own addictive piercing into her daughter's dating behavior. Both women can master the debilitating belief of, *The mother must take charge of a grown daughter's attitudes about a possible relationship with a man.*

If this introspective approach doesn't work with her mother, who continues her rigid inquiries, the daughter can respond with Eddie's hand-raising command *Stop!* If *Stop!* doesn't work, the daughter walks into another room.

In short, critical thinking requires us to observe and feel, and jumps to center stage with responsibility and action, which includes inquiry and, if necessary, a meditative silence providing answers.

When we become more consciously aware of what's inside and around us, we experience ourselves as an *expression of consciousness-energy*—and smile or chortle when we see our brief descent into ego-based self-distress.

Conscious awareness also opens a door to, *What is my purpose in this life?* With greater self-examination, we inquire into *What do I want . . . Where do I find it? . . . What are the steps to becoming it? . . . Who can help me achieve my purpose?* I hope that some readers put this book on a shelf and then meditate for a month about these life-changing italicized questions.

Almost everyone has the capacity to edge up from base awareness (lower or conditioned self) into more conscious awareness (higher Self). If a person makes this transition, he or she will cultivate greater self-confidence and probably make more money. My father worked for his father, who was the greatest handball player in the world in 1910 and possessed a domineering nature. Dad wasn't happy working for his ever-controlling father. Finally becoming cognizant about his father's use-'em-up attitude toward his four sons, Dad released his neediness for fatherly approval and asserted himself by establishing his own business at age thirty-nine. He finally mastered a vision of steady work for a good salary, work that didn't involve driving a truck twice a week from his father's ice cream company four hundred miles down and then back up the Central Valley of California. In sum, my father in his work career transformed from an unhappy *conditioned* state to a happier *growing up* state.

Relax about your spiritual practice. Take pleasure in small shifts away from *shoulds* and *should nots.* This conversion is similar to intelligent dieting. For the first month, no soft drinks such as sugary Coke or Pepsi. During the second month, slow down on fried foods until, at month's end, you're off them for good. The third month eliminates eating after 7:00 p.m. Like dieting, *slow, small, and steady* is a good mantra for executing variations of OFRA. The goal is to embrace both our inside and outside worlds so that they coordinate with and complete each other.

Two Meditations and Two Exercises Employing OFRA

Hundreds of worthwhile action practices exist to complete OFRA. Number two and three below are better identified as "exercises" than meditations. I suggest that you practice each of these four for two or three days and then use the one that best serves you. All four can guide us to more consistent mindfulness. Each is simple. Each is doable. Each is powerfully effective as a remedy for our hurtful reactions based on largely hidden belief systems.

Real-Time OFRA

#1 Gratitude Breath Meditation

Breathe in any add-on, such as procrastination, and breathe out gratitude for observing it. We can breathe in *I feel guilt about my laziness* and breathe out *I am grateful that I am steadily taking action about my procrastination.*

2 A Physical Activity

You can do a physical activity such as laughing, growling, or singing a verse to tone down an irritation about something. For example, suppose that nature is intruding on an activity. On the in-breathe and then the out-breath, stomp the ground with one foot each time you say each word in the following sentence. *Rain stopped my golfing with Samuel.*

3 A Communication Exercise About What You Want and Don't Want

You feel abused and put down when your lady roughly says, "Abel, why haven't you uncorked the wine bottles?" You reply, "Sweetheart, please say whatever you want to say, but say it in a friendly tone." Notice that you're saying precisely what you want and don't want, but in a kind manner. No words can express the profound benefits of an authentic practice of this one exercise. The *doing* of this exercise leads to *being* the friendly independence that we all regard as sacred. Whole books have been written about "communicating well," but this one paragraph is sufficient if you practice it bit by bit, steadily.

4 Sit-Down OFRA

Suppose that you're a waiter and you've just finished with a customer who has pressed you for two hours with a tornado of requests. You've met them all in a friendly manner. Now he's leaving through the front door. You pick up the bill and his cash. This tough customer hasn't left you a single penny for a tip.

Your add-on is frustrated anger. This type of discourtesy has happened before, but never with a customer you've served so well for so long. You notice that this anger haunts you for a few minutes, much more than fifteen seconds classifying it as a casual or natural response to irritating behaviors. So you do one of the three real-time meditations or exercises described in Real-Time OFRA above. These can reduce your anger but not resolve your issue with the discourteous customer. You don't have the time to carry out a twenty minute sit-down meditation to better comprehend your frustration. Therefore, you wait until you're home to do a sit-down meditation that can jump you out of this emotional trap.

You might want a timer for this meditation. Choose the number of minutes for each part of the meditation that best suits you.

> Assume a meditative posture of sitting in a chair with your back straight, feet planted on the floor, and hands relaxed on your lap. Consciously breathe in and out until you arrive at a tranquil state.
>
> • Observation. Read out loud any notes you've taken. Picture in your mind the disturbing feelings that occurred earlier in the day.
> • Feeling. Let the most dominant negative emotions completely arise, even if you have to

scream and curse. Slowly, deeply, breathe in and out to calm yourself.

- Take responsibility. Ask yourself, *Is this a response or a reaction? Have I blamed the customer for my negativity? Or did I blame myself for this add-on? Or did I accept responsibility for my negative reaction?*

Verbally or silently ask yourself, *Is there a long-term negative belief that created my add-on?*

- Take action. Rest in silence that provides authentic answers to, *Is there a long-term unrealistic belief that created my add-on of frustrated anger?* Do nothing but observe your breathing. The silence might answer something like, *Unrealistic beliefs? Everyone has an ample budget for good tipping . . . or, If I perform well, they always will give me a good tip.*

If you receive an *Aha!* answer from the silence, good for you. If not, redo this meditation once each day until the answer arrives. Now you'll rest in the satisfaction that you're successfully training your mind to serve you, not hurt you. Any restaurant worker is better off when he or she detaches from add-ons triggered by customers. The identical process can work for teachers bothered by students, trainers upset by clients, doctors irritated by patients or work conditions, or workers stressed by coworkers or bosses.

> Your final action is to write down the questions, emotions, and insights that you have about the core negative belief dishing out add-ons.

You might be asking yourself, "How is 'rest in silence' and 'observe my breathing' an *action?*" I define an action as "a behavior directed toward a result." In this sense, the process of sitting without movement, observing your breathing, asking a question of the silence, and resting in silence for an answer are actions leading to new, fresh, revealing insights. Questioning and then silence are actions practiced around the world with inquiry meditation. When we're plagued by an emotional issue (an add-on), we can resolve it through sit-down inquiry meditation.

Ask a friend to meet with you at the end of the first week of practicing these real-time and sit-down meditations. Share your notes, ideas, and feelings with this person.

You might discover that your beliefs and their add-ons are making you kind of crazy. If so, write down your impressions about your unrealistic expectations of others and yourself. A small percentage of people are real bastards. The server waited on one in his restaurant. His cleansing question is, *Why did I get so upset with this customer? I serve a bastard once in a while. Why did I take it personally?*

When the silence finally divulges an answer, treat yourself to a high-quality restaurant, swimming at the beach or river, or a ticket to your favorite sports event or theater. Repeat to yourself in your own words something like, "I'm *seeing* my crazy, unrealistic expectations. They're just conditioning that I can steadily eradicate." Or scribble down your own wording about this truth: *Emotional growth requires a weirdly uncomfortable phase. May I have patience with peeking into my long-term beliefs.*

Chapter Summary

Authoritarians and despots would hate this chapter. It sums up *A Creative Toolkit of Meditations'* resolutions for stress elimination. How can a control-freak parent, spouse, employer, or politician govern the behavior of stress-free individuals? The less stress we have, the more we behave independently and authentically.

The prerequisite for stressless mindfulness is OFRA: observation, feeling, responsibility, action. OFRA is achieved by slowing down, asking a question, resting in silence, receiving an answer, and perhaps taking brief notes. With OFRA, we evolve from *thinkers* into *knowers*.

The first three meditations or exercises are real-time; the last is sit-down. The real-time activities are gratitude breath meditation, physical action, and friendly communication about what you want and don't want. The sit-down meditation employs OFRA's four steps.

If we had only one tool to gain mindfulness, it would be OFRA, which is pure manifestation of critical thinking. Critical thinking is essential for solving any personal issue. One superb action is to master friendly requests for what we want and a friendly no for what we don't want.

Like good dieting and exercising, OFRA can be arrived at with a slow, small, steady approach.

Section 2

WAKING UP

Chapter Four

WAKING UP TO *WHAT YOU ARE*

> Absolute unmixed attention is prayer.
> Simone Weil

An Awakening or Enlightenment Experience

For the five weeks prior to my awakening, I endured an unhappy dreariness after I'd understood that my true identity had nothing to do with any beliefs. The more I examined my beliefs and their add-ons through meditations and OFRA, the more I understood that that all of them were illusions. All my beliefs, personal, worldly, or spiritual—whether positive or negative—had been my guiding god, my cornerstone in negotiating with my culture. I'd lost all my convictions that I was a good guy, a helpful lover, a great teacher. Of course, I still experienced thoughts about these convictions, but I now knew that they had nothing to do with me, my still unknown essence. My true identity had nothing at all to do with my beliefs, which seemed real but were pure illusions.

One day I was doing a Buddhist meditation by inhaling, *I am a conduit for the heart to reach all things,* and exhaling, *All beings are a part of me.* As I was looking out the living room window at trees and buildings, the recognition *I Am Consciousness* blew up my mind. This recognition was similar to an earlier satori at a Zen center but far more extensive and explosive. In addition, it cast a new light on my emotional self.

One after another, *realizations* or *knowings* swept away the old *me.* These realizations, recognitions, or knowings are described below. The first sentences cite my actual recognitions, and the italicized sentences represent my thoughts that followed these recognitions. For sixty minutes after my spiritual blow-up, I wrote down these recognitions and ideas. They arrived one after another, in the order written below.

Consciousness is universal.
Everyone has consciousness as the source of experiences. We can't smell a flower without consciousness. Can't think a single thought or feel anything without consciousness.

Now I can observe, clearly see, all my negative thoughts and feelings . . . as well as all my positive thoughts and feelings.
Nothing inside is hidden.

Clarity makes me more humble.
How can I be arrogant if I'm noticing all my garbage, from a supposed superior-sounding voice to a "You're wrong!" attitude toward someone?

The mind is only an expression of consciousness.
Thoughts and feelings are just as concrete and intermittent as the other five senses. Negative emotions can pass away as quickly as any taste of chocolate or touch of my hairbrush.

Oneness unites me with everything. Everything is interconnected.
Consciousness allows me to experience and thus be unified with my world around me. Without consciousness, nothing can occur. So . . . if I am consciousness, I can experience a cough or a tree. I feel the cough in my throat and lungs, an explosion inside my chest. I feel the tree bark on my hands. I am the cough or the tree, the chest explosion. Now I know what all the spiritual books mean when they talk about oneness.

I'm distinct from anything or anyone else.
My consciousness is experiencing a world distinct from that of anyone else that has ever lived or ever will live. Has anyone ever seen this exact configuration, colors, and sizes of leaves and grasses, for exactly as long as I've watched them? I've never before grasped that I'm distinct from anything else yet also interconnected with everything. Weird and magical. All-embracing.

My identities have been based on my beliefs, judgments, evaluations, and any labeling of myself as related to others.
Formerly, I was lost without these beliefs. Now I love this lack of beliefs. Even if useful, the contents of beliefs are illusions.

Consciousness has no judgments or pressures infecting it.
I am consciousness eliminates emotional attachment to anything. Emotions are more huge, but not taking me out of present time.

I am consciousness is a recognition, not an insight.
I am consciousness is not just an insight. Insights clarify me. Recognitions change me.

Consciousness has zero strain.
Zero effort. It's pure knowing without thinking about it, without trying to be a good boy or impress someone. Gotta be a good boy is a belief and my beliefs are gone. I'll be a good boy whenever I want to be.

Knowing I am consciousness will enable me to express more emotion.
I won't identity myself as my emotions. I can appreciate being happy or sad without judgment that I should be happy or sad. Compassion for myself and others is a constant.

Now I understand what freedom is.
No expectations. No need to be some way. No stress to be something other than what I am right now.

We're all equal because we're all consciousness.
Anything less than consciousness drains respect from, "We are equal."

I won't brood over issues. I'll meditate them to oblivion.
Will I still have issues to confront? Yes! No big deal. Much easier to handle them.

Those were my recognitions and thoughts/feelings/ sensations for the sixty minutes after my awakening. They're still resonating and, even if not quite as intense, fully alive. Life is . . . well, I don't have words for it. "Wow!" is my best verbal pointer. Awesome! Tasty!

A month later, I wrote the sentences below. They rephrase the traits of my enlightenment after truth blasted away my conceptual shell. Other people's awakening could manifest differently.

- Consciousness is I and me.
- I am interconnected with everything. Everything is interconnected with everything.
- I am unique in my experiencing of life.
- I observe my inner world's hidden negative beliefs. Therefore, I can't be anything less than humble.
- Before awakening, some seekers can go through a "dark night" of losing their identities.
- "I am consciousness" is not a common *insight* but a life-changing *recognition*.
- A belief is real; it happens. However, its *contents* are illusions (e.g., ethnicity, racism, sexism, good, bad).
- Enlightenment is freedom from all beliefs. *Knowing* is contextual (holistically overarching, here and now, intuitive not linear, and not based upon norms). No attachments.
- Enlightenment is *awe* at the nature of everything around us, an *awe* beyond language, a stupendous vastness manifesting as us.

- All humans are equal because we're all consciousness. That is, if our definition of consciousness includes energy. If not, then we're all consciousness-energy.

The Language and Science of the Awake State

Our silent minds access information from the no-limits field of universal intelligence, what certain theologians call the "mind of God."

Many overlapping terms point toward ineffable spiritual realities. Below are thirteen typical terms associated with enlightenment. These terms are the meat and bones of spiritual inquiry. What's the best word or phrase for What We Are, our essence, our true nature, our source of sources? Most practitioners would say awareness or spirit, but my vote is consciousness.

If the word *consciousness* in the declaration *I am consciousness* doesn't strike you as appropriate for what you are, you can embrace one of the words below. All of them have been widely used by sages and mystics to point toward What We Are. They're cited here because I don't want to force my favorite term, consciousness, down your psyche. Decide which word, or words, suit you best.

Essence (What I Am) terms:

1. *Awareness* (everyone uses it).
2. *Silence* (Sufism).
3. *Void* (Buddhism)
4. *Nothingness* (Eastern sects, Christian Meister Eckhart)
5. *Emptiness* (Eastern sects)

6. *The light* (Quakerism) or *The Light and Information* (Matrix Energetics)
7. *Witness* (many writers)
8. *Knowing* (many writers)
9. *Presence* (common term)
10. *Here and now* (common term).
11. *Consciousness* (used in both Eastern and Western practices)
12. *Spirit* (Christianity, Vedanta Hinduism, and Zen Buddhism)
13. *Flow* (a current popular word)

Void, nothingness, and emptiness can imply blankness or nonexistence. That meaning does not apply to the spiritual nature of these three terms. Instead, they point to the connotations of *total vastness, complete and uncomplicated clarity,* and *absolutely unimpeded.*

If you recognize one or more of these qualities as your eternal essence, your whole viewpoint can shift toward increased conscious awareness and even enlightenment itself. A mystic is someone who authentically and intuitively *knows* what he or she *is* and *lives out that knowing.*

You've probably noticed that I emphasize the role of silence in spiritual practice. *Everyone accesses silence to some degree and in some way or another.* With silence, we obtain the *knowing* of the mystic. I had an insight recently about silence's value in evangelical Christianity. Evangelists have an intimate connection with Jesus. Evangelists ask Jesus for advice about what's pestering them. An evangelical man might ask Jesus, "Lord, I'm short of money, but I need some pants. What do I do?" Now his mind goes silent as he waits for an answer. Then his silence speaks to him with "You have one good pair of slacks and two okay pairs of jeans. But your bathing suit is ragged. The girls at the complex's pool won't have a good opinion of you. Buy a new swimming suit." The evangelical now thinks (or says) something like, *Thank you, Jesus. To honor you, I'll clean up the church yard next Sunday.*

Of course, evangelicals entreat Jesus to assist them with far more threatening situations than my pallid swimming suit example. The male evangelist so far has employed Jesus only to gain *knowing* about one minor aspect of his relationship with women. A year later, he might ask, "Dear Lord, Should I marry her?" That's a critical item to *know*.

A description of the mystical or awake state is found in *The Essential Ken Wilber: An Introductory Reader*. Wilber writes, "The essence of mysticism is that in the deepest part of your own being, in the very center of your own pure awareness, you are fundamentally one with Spirit, one with Godhead, one with the All, in a timeless and eternal fashion." For me, this elegant language captures the experience of *knowing* What We Are.

In his book *Quantum Questions*, Wilber compares the written works of the greatest physicists of the twentieth century and shows that most of them were exemplary mystics: Einstein, Heisenberg, Schrodinger, de Broglie, Planck, Bohr, Pauli, Eddington, and Jeans (all Nobel laureates except two). Science is often viewed as contradictory to orthodox religious doctrines, but the great majority of the most innovative modern physicists align with mysticism or the enlightened state. Wilber quotes Schrodinger, a Nobel laureate for his exploration of quantum physics.

> It is not possible that this unity of knowledge, feeling, and choice that you call your own should have sprung into being from nothingness at a given moment not so long ago; rather, this knowledge,

feeling, and choice are essentially eternal and unchangeable and numerically one in all men, nay, in all sentient beings . . . for eternally and always there is only now, one and the same now; the present is the only thing that has no end.

What a paradox! Three hundred years of classical Newtonian cause-effect science pitted itself against the limitations of religious doctrines; in sharp contrast, modern quantum physics marches in step with ancient and modern mysticism, the intuitive *knowing* of our oneness with the All.

Schrodinger appears to be a mystic who favors the term now or presence as a pointer to What I Am.

The following paraphrase by Wilber of sage Sri Ramana Maharshi's writing about awareness echoes the above descriptions.

The one thing we are always aware of is . . . awareness itself. We already have basic awareness, in the form of the capacity to Witness whatever arises . . . As the old Zen master used to say, 'You hear the birds? You see the sun? Who is not enlightened?' None of us can even imagine a state where basic awareness is not, because we would still be aware of imagining. Even in dreams we are aware. Moreover, these traditions maintain that there are not two different types of awareness, enlightened versus ignorant. There is only awareness. And this awareness, exactly and precisely as it is, without corrections or modifications at all, is itself Spirit, since there is nowhere Spirit is not.

Sri Ramana Maharshi plucks *Witness, awareness* and *spirit* as his choice descriptors for enlightenment.

The body-mind of all animals manifests consciousness which, in humans, enables our body-mind to evolve a self that can witness itself as unique and separate from other body-minds. In sum, consciousness is an eternal, primordial awareness that exists prior to all experiencing and *is required* for all experiencing.

Consciousness as source allows us to see, hear, smell, touch, taste, think, and have emotions. We can realize that consciousness fosters our self as an evolutionary survival mechanism. Awakening to ourselves as consciousness leads to our recognition that *all* beliefs are imaginary constructions that don't actually exist. Now we're free from them. The phrase *must have and be [consciousness]to experience anything* equally applies to all terms for what we call our *essence: awareness, silence, void, nothingness, emptiness, the light, witness, knower, presence, here and now, spirit, flow.*

- I must have and be awareness to experience anything.
- I must have and be nothingness to experience anything.
- I must have and be the light to experience anything.
- I must have and be here and now to experience anything.
- I must have and be spirit to experience anything.

Yes, we must comprehend that *any* term for our source is dicey. One Eastern sect calls God "The Inexpressible." Good for it! For me, consciousness works best because other words edge toward something tangible and thus are more limited. In most of our minds, "God" is a word for a deity that creates everything and thus is somehow apart from everything. "Essence" suggests some kind of quality or trait. "Unity" dodges uniqueness. The dictionary definition of "awareness" stresses the notion of "awareness of something," not "source" of all. You can play with these words and their dictionary meanings. For me, *I am consciousness* has zero personal defining traits yet implies that everything is fully, amazingly, experienced through a single source.

Barriers to Realizing *I Am Consciousness*

If we think, *I'm in danger of starving* or *I'm in danger of being abandoned* or *I'm in danger of being discriminated against,* and these possibilities *actually* exist, these thoughts identify a reality that needs to be addressed. Our brains are working real-time. If we think, *I'm not smart enough to do that project* or *I have to do what Kate wants*, we're probably assaulted by an unconscious belief system that blocks out our true identity, our sense of Self. Once we recognize this belief as negative and limiting, we can commence processing it out of our nervous system.

Our first journey is *maturing* or *growing up*, becoming a confident, competent, caring adult. Here we learn to observe and become introspective, consciously experiencing our add-ons and their underlying beliefs. Presenting us with diverse contexts to explore and master, growing up never ends. Meditation on *Who am I?* helps us to grow up, as do psychotherapy, retreats, weekly discussion groups, interactive dialogue with intelligent friends, or any combination of these prompts.

Our second journey is *waking up*, spiritual enlightenment or awakening. We can use the meditative tool of inquiring *What am I?* to achieve an answer. These two journeys can reinforce each other.

Nevertheless, people are often biased against waking up. Most people steer clear of *What am I?* They shield themselves against *What am I?* inquiry by attachment to their jobs, romantic entanglements, family duties, sports fandom, religious creed orientations—all of which are strong suits that enrich our lives but also armor us from deeper commitment to inquiry. However, when we crawl into *What am I?* the habitual answers such as *family man, spiritual seeker, credit manager, pretty girl,* or *tough guy* lose resonance. Diligently pursued, *What am I?* refuses to be subsumed by these culture-driven identities. This persistent What am I? inquiry can cause us to feel that something is incomplete, forged, or wounded in our lives. A not-quite-thereness pervades us.

Lucid not-quite-thereness is prompted by growing up to the fact that we have limiting beliefs. We discover that we're becoming more intelligently functional, yet *something incomplete* digs into us. Buddhist teachers have jokingly claimed that we typically endure six thousand judgmental thoughts each day.

Why do many meditators experience, even after years of practice, this soft yet pervasive incompleteness?

One answer is that all humans are exposed to some degree of negativity. As described in chapters 1 to 3, our nervous systems unwittingly absorb negative beliefs when we're children. Recent research indicates that approximately 50 percent of our ingrained negative attitudes derive from our genetic makeup, while the other 50 percent originate with our family and culture. Of course, we're also blessed with positive genetic and acquired beliefs.

A second answer is that meditative tools and mantras themselves can become an elusive, cunning species of add-on. They can become the issue, not the solution. The paradox is that, although *growing up* is necessary for awakening, growing-up exercises can degenerate into conditioned beliefs, such as *I have to practice this meditation in order to be happy*. This limiting quality can occur with meditation, relationships, political affiliation, religious belief, and culturally assigned identities.

An example of a devilishly subtle limitation is my favorite pre-enlightenment mantra of *relax*. If I mentally fumed, *Darn it, I have to listen to Joe pontificating at the party tonight*, I'd breathe in that thought and breathe out, *Relax*. Now I was fine with myself. I wasn't worried about disrupting Joe's rampage at every liberal policy since the Declaration of Independence. What I hadn't understood is that my *relax* self-command was itself slowly degenerating, due to my belief *I am unworthy and must be vigilant*, into the add-on, *Keep doing the relax mantra*. After a while, this mantra didn't work, and I finally identified it as an add-on.

The next afternoon, I did a long meditation about *relax*, and all my convictions about mantras collapsed. In a sense, mantras and meditations are *strong suits*, attitudes and behaviors that benefit us in some ways and bedevil us in other ways. I had known for decades that emotional attachment to a guru was a problem, not a solution. Now I understood that attachment to a mantra (*relax*) also can become a problem, albeit one with many positive benefits.

In this hour-long meditation, I discovered that any constant striving to be present and be consciously aware had both lifted me up the emotional-spiritual mountain and pushed me into a deep hole on this mountain's plateau. My bond with my meditative regimen was yet another form of unnecessary, reactive *thinking*. My practice had gifted me with self-assurance, an emotional haven. However, *attachment* to my mantra, *Be consciously aware*, had diminished my aliveness to here and now.

Most of us require a moderate emotional attachment to a mantra or to meditation before we transcend our attachment to it, just like overeaters require an absolute dedication to a strict diet before they master proper eating. Their dedication, now less necessary, eases up. At this point, the reformed overeater can bite by bite enjoy her food without any urge to gulp it down. She eats properly because she *wants to*, not because she *has to*. Reactivity can change to *response*. Now the mantra is no longer necessary.

Is meditation essential for liberation? Yes! Is any *striving* to carry out a meditative practice liberating? No! However, a hopefully short initial period of willful striving might be necessary. Growing up practitioners might need an inner voice telling them, *Do it!* As we hike toward waking up, that voice fades out.

Since this meditation, I'm home in my inner world as I observe my nonpresence and return to full connection with the outer world. I call this mode of responsiveness *freedom*.

Watch Out for Subtle Addiction to "I"

Meditation has a second addictive barrier. One afternoon after my awakening I was forced to stop using the term "I" in some meditations. I was sitting on the couch and breathing in, *I love myself*, and breathing out, *I constantly express my love for everything*. After seven or eight in-and-out breaths, something put a *Stop!* to this meditation. *What's happening?* I asked myself, and quickly the answer came. *Too many "I's." "I can't use "I" in any meditation. There is no "I." "I" am consciousness itself, and the "I" or self is a necessary but nonexisting fabrication.*

So I substituted *consciousness* for the "I" of *I love myself* and the "I" of *I continuously express love for everything.* For several in-and-out breaths, consciousness seemed awkward but then sparkled with meaning. It was as if my awakening had seeped into every cell of my body, and my body had been sealed in invisible gold to prevent the leakage of any aspect of the awake state.

If your favorite term for *What I am* is *Witness* (a popular term among seekers), your language might evolve from *I love myself* to *The witness loves itself.* Can you feel the power of that mantra just by reading it? Instead of "I," you can employ each of the thirteen essence terms in your meditations.

To summarize this book's approach, the growing up *Who am I?* investigation of our often narcissistic self can shift us toward greater equanimity, love, and emotional connectedness. We must pick our way through the burning coals of negative beliefs before we fully engage waking up's *What am I?* For me, the resolution is discovered in Jack Kornfield's phrase about perceptions: "the flow of consciousness that experiences them all."

"Experiencing everything" is phrased by some Buddhist writers as "endarkenment." We profit from experiencing our dark side—rowdiness, weakness, confusion, inane anger, poor judgment—as an incorporation into wholeness. We honor our dark nature by bringing it into the light in order to transcend it. Our darkness is our guide and teacher.

Ken Wilber's magnificent mantra *"Include and transcend"* suggests the triumphs of both growing up and waking up. *Include* is the intention of growing up—*transcend* is the intention of waking up.

Three Meditations on *What I Am*

Real-Time Meditation on Consciousness

This real-time meditation is best practiced in the morning or afternoon for ten to fifteen minutes, or more if desired. First you select a setting, such as your tabletop at a meal. Seated there, you ask yourself, *What is required for me to experience four or five particular items of this setting?* Ask this question with different wordings and address different senses, as shown in the following examples:

> Step one: Select a setting. If you're at your desk, ask yourself, *What does it take for me to experience this pencil? This pen? This desktop? Or anything else?*

> If you're walking down the street, ask yourself, *How is it possible for me to feel my feet striking the ground?* Or, *How is it possible for me to watch that car driving alongside me?* or *How is it possible for me to be so delighted with this fresh breeze caressing my face?*

> Step two: After each question, drop all thoughts and enter into the silence for a minute or two. When you're ready to drive, ask yourself, *What is required for me to feel this steering wheel?*—>silence. *See this dashboard?*—>silence. *Hear the engine?*—>silence. *See the driveway?*—>silence. Of course, make sure that you're in neutral drive, have your brakes on, and someone isn't sitting beside you wondering, *What's this weird guy doing?*

When you're sitting on your couch and thinking, ask yourself, *What allows me to think I'm tired.*—>silence, or to think, *I can't learn East Coast swing.*—>silence, or to think, *My co-workers are fine people.*—>silence.

You'll see, hear, touch, taste, smell, and think about four to eight objects in any particular setting. In summary, pick one setting, locate an object in that setting, and ask the question, *How is it possible for me to experience [whatever]?* Then, for a minute or two, experience this object and then switch to another object, then another, then another, in that same setting.

Step three: When step two is finished, slowly and deeply breathe in, "*What is required for me to experience anything?*" Now, stay in silence for several minutes.

Sit-down Meditation on Consciousness

This sitting meditation takes fifteen to twenty minutes—or an hour—once a day. It could be done later in the day after doing the real-time meditation in the morning or afternoon. In different wording, it's asking the same question as the above real-time meditation. There's only one question leading to awakening, and every tradition phrases it uniquely. Many contemplative monks have practiced a version of this meditation for years.

1. Sit in meditation posture, with your feet firmly on the floor, back straight, shoulders back, and head level.

2. For a couple of minutes, relax into a calm mind state during which you fully experience whatever arises and feel the peaceful, perhaps vibratory, spaciousness in your upper body.

3. Now ask yourself, "What am I?" on the in-breath and relax even more into empty peacefulness. Let in whatever answer pops up, but then very gently *release* it with the out-breath.

    If a random thought interrupts, ask yourself "What am I?"

4. Carry out this sequence for the remainder of your fifteen to twenty minutes. You can write out any insights or answers as they occur or after the meditation is finished. For each answer, breathe it in with a long, slow, deep breath, and breathe it out again with a long, slow, deep breath.

5. To finish, jot down which answer best expresses *What I am*. Thank the silence for any fresh answers. If no answer comes up, thank the silence for an answer presented in future meditations.

Meditation on Unity and Oneness

If this meditation blows you away, exclusively practice it. Don't do it when driving or walking across a street with passing cars.

Eight to ten times a day, or more, for a week or a month be mindful about particular experiences. After each one, think or say, *I am [whatever the object or focal point of that experience is]*.

Examples:

Be mindful of the sky. Then think or say
I <u>am</u> the sky above.

Observe a tree. Then think or say,
I am the leafy lushness of that tree.

Look at a lady (or a man), and think or say,
I am the feeling she (he) is sooo curvy when she's (he's) standing.

If you have pain in your left shoulder, think or say,
I am the soreness of the left shoulder.

Note that the *am* is underlined for emphasis. This emphasis might enhance or detract from the unity experience. According to your needs, emphasize *am* or not.

A second variation of this meditation is to identify the *quality* of your experiences. If you're shuffling around your living room with music driving you, you can phrase the *I am* statement in this fashion:

I am the movements of this dancing.
I am the delicate vibrating piano chords of this dancing.
I am the solid floor permitting this dancing.
I am the infinite movements of my dancing.
I am the spaciousness this dancing endlessly opens up.

As always, mindfully perform each of these three meditations until one draws you into a month or two of steady practice. If none of these three result in enjoyable experiences, that's okay. Staying with a healthy diet can take a while before you look at your dinner plate with a smile.

Chapter Summary

One day when you're barbecuing a steak or vacuuming the floor, you might have an enlightenment experience. Without meditating, that experience might not have happened. Or something else entirely different might open the doorway. There's no A—>B—>C pattern to spiritual practice and change. I've told my story, but other cogent stories might be quite different.

"Enlightenment" has several synonyms, including "awake" and "self-realized." Common terms relating to traits resulting from an enlightenment experience are unity, oneness, silence, interconnectedness, detachment from negativity, and freedom.

Life is easier after awakening. We more easily express ourselves or choose to say nothing. Something indescribable but much more vibrant and consequential than "mind" and "thoughts" lives inside and through us. We respect others' capacities and get by without negative judgments. We're all equal. Others have the same awake nature as we do; some simply haven't yet realized what they are. With our new lucidity, we recognize that every person we encounter possesses a skill or two that we lack. In addition, awakening's gift of close observation of our own negative traits is humbling.

As this chapter says, no one grows up 100 percent. Likewise, everyone in some way has mastered a few tactics for dipping into silence.

According to Ken Wilber's evidence, many great physicists walk the mystical path. Quantum physics seems to encourage the mystical state of inner silence, oneness, and interdependence.

We can limit ourselves by overstriving for spiritual change, by excessive dedication to a particular practice or mantra, or by fixation on improving "me" or "I." Indeed, "me" and "I" are illusions.

Enlightenment does require that we observe and feel our dark emotions and habits.

If we desire a single phrase to encompass our journey to awakenening, it might be "include and transcend."

Section 3

INTEGRATING GROWING UP AND WAKING UP

Chapter Five

INVESTIGATIVE DIALOGUE SERVING OURSELVES AND OTHERS

Craft must have clothes, but truth loves to go naked.
Gnomologia

The Value of Investigative Dialogue

How do we achieve mindfulness with others and with ourselves? One key component is investigative dialogue, a core aspect of an authentic friendship, relationship, or good work environment. It's a skill that we all potentially possess.

Investigative dialogue involves (1) personally relating to your speech partner's issue, (2) empathically listening, and (3) inquiring. When this trio happens, we become investigative dialoguers. With inquiry, we penetrate into our partner's subterranean *why* of the issue being discussed. *Why* questioning shoots an arrow into the buried, conditioned beliefs ingrained in us.

In the movie *The King's Speech*, Lionel is the speech therapist hired to cure Britain's King Bertie's psychologically induced stuttering. Lionel portrays a master investigative dialoguer who relates to the issue of Bertie's stuttering, empathically listens, and deeply inquires into Bertie's stuttering. Possessing vast listening capacity, Lionel also effortlessly inquires into Bertie's fear of rejection so that his stuttering can end. I view King Bertie as the main character of this film and Lionel as the ultimate opponent who wins out by utilizing investigative dialogue. He's Merlin listening to King Arthur.

Do we require investigative dialogue all the time? *No!* It's important maybe one conversation out of ten or fifteen. Most conversations are mainly chitchat, like a partner rapping about her cat's recent indigestion. If the listener inquires, "How long did your kitty have indigestion?" the speaker may pause for a moment and then say, "Well . . . I should have taken her to the vet a week ago."

Now, with the listener saying only, "Hmm. One week!," the speaker might admit her guilt with, "Yes, a full week. I don't feel good about not taking her in sooner."

This dialogue might segue into self-blaming about improper caring for animals. Let's hope not. Much better if investigative dialogue can help a partner discover his or her *motives*. Sophie and I are big-league motive-seekers. We're grateful for this inquiry boost in our relationship. If we maintain our investigative dialogue skills, no unhappiness or need for a therapist.

Trait One of Investigative Dialogue: Relating to the Issue

When a friend presents an issue, do you follow the discussion or do you think about other topics? If a partner is relating her unhappiness with her mother-in-law, do you think, *Poor soul! My mother-in-law has something like her mother-in-law's controlling nature.* Or you might wonder, *Why does any forty-year-old adult care what a mother-in-law thinks?* Neither of these two thoughts directly relates to the speaker's issue. They're only your perspectives. Little empathy and connectedness exist. More appropriate thoughts are, *She is really upset* or *She could resolve this crushing problem.*

To fully relate to the topic, to listen, and then to inquire, we must shut down our random thoughts. *Any* conversation can become a useful spiritual exercise of silencing our minds.

In October of my second year teaching at a community college, a star halfback in my writing class told me that the football coach was furious at him.

"Why?" I asked.

"Because I'm taking your class. You treat players just like anyone else. If they don't learn to write well, you give them a D or F. You're on the blacklist."

"What's the blacklist?"

He grimaced. "A list of teachers to avoid. Coach tells us, 'Don't take his class!'"

Intrigued, I asked my third question, "So why are you taking my class?" He paused for a while before answering, "Football! I want to write about playing football. When I get older and quit doing football, I want to become a broadcaster, so I got to get my writing better."

I reflected a moment before finishing off with, "For your research paper, interview three broadcasters about how playing football will help you become a broadcaster. What's their opinion about the relationship between being an athlete and becoming a sports broadcaster?"

Instead of smiling, he hesitated. In a fretful voice he said, "But will they listen to me? Those guys are all pros, and I'm just a freshman at college."

"We'll figure out the questions when we have a session on your research paper."

"I'll do it!"

I related to his issue because he was my student and because he was deeply interested in his future career. This halfback earned a B in my course and wrote a good research paper after interviewing three broadcasters.

If you're not relating to your partner's issue, here are three workable remedies:

- Recall your discomfort with a similar situation.
- Recognize that you care enough about your partner to listen to what he is saying.
- Say to yourself, *In what way does this issue concern me?*

Trait Two of Investigative Dialogue: Three Styles of Listening

Madelyn Burley-Allen in her highly read book *Listening: The Forgotten Skill,* describes three styles of listening. After Sophie and I had absorbed Burley-Allen's three styles, our conversations grew wider and deeper.

- Empathic listening.
- Hearing words but not really listening.
- Shifting back and forth from empathic listening to not listening while prepping our own responses.

A) Empathic Listening

The most worthy style is *empathic listening.* We forget ourselves and enter into mental silence that permits us to read our partner's mind and soul. With her overassertive speech, is she trying to impress us to cover up a self-image problem underlying her prideful words? Or does she want to unload? Or to hear our insights about her issue? Because of our eye contact, body movements, and short, concise comments and questions, the speaker is reassured that we're empathically listening.

Empathic listening can be achieved by using what I call the "facilitator trick" of always siding with the speaker. If someone at a party sponsored by our apartment complex says, "I don't like the management here," I'll show my potential agreement with, "Interesting! Why so?" Despite my openness to agreement with my partner, I'm certain that our complex's management has both positive and negative attributes. If a lunch group member claims, "America is the greatest country in the world," I'll initially side with that statement by asking, "How does that play out?" I won't project my conviction that America has amazingly great qualities but also a history of imperialistic harshness.

Why do I suggest walking beside others' beliefs? *People don't like being told what to feel or do. They don't like being made to feel wrong or inferior.* We need to facilitate in a nonjudgmental way, not to act like a swaggering expert. We can only suggest, not dictate. "You might consider . . ." enlarges our dialogue, but not, "The best way is . . ."

Can we edge the speaker into apprehending the issue that's torturing him or her? Yes, if we're aware from the get-go that we're directing the conversation toward the *why?* of the speaker's issue. My student had violated the dictate of his football coach, often a demigod for players. The coach focused primarily on players devoting themselves to winning. He didn't have much concern about the *whys* of players preparing for a worthwhile career.

With empathic listening, we shed our add-ons during dialoguing. Good! Our silent mind hears what our partner is delivering, and then this sacred silence can respond with a thoughtful question or comment. Empathic listening cultivates our ability to serve others. When we bless others with our attention, we become pleasurably connected with them.

In all cases, inquirers should never impose upon speech partners. The speaker should experience them as empathetic. We can ask ourselves, *Am I feeling what my partner is saying, putting myself in her shoes?* We can announce, "I *got* it!" to indicate that we have carefully listened and haven't become lost in the speaker's story. With empathic listening, we're tuned into the speaker's intention, yet we're still fully aware of our own stance, or bias, about the issue discussed.

B) Hearing Words But Not Really Listening

Madelyn Burley-Allen's second style of listening is, "hearing words but not really listening."

Style two listening isn't empathic. We understand what the speaker's words mean yet aren't motivated to perceive the speaker's *intention*. At a recent family dinner, James sat across from me. His wife, Patty, sat at the end of the table to my left. James asked, "What did you and Sophie do on your Seattle trip?" I began describing the awesome cleanliness and elegant architectural features of Seattle homes and buildings. For a moment or two, he appeared to be listening empathically, and then, after a waiter briefly interrupted us by placing Patty's dessert next to his, he switched to rapping about TV shows with a male family member seated at his left.

James had listened to my words, but not to my intention, which was to testify that Seattle's two million people had created amazingly similar, clean, and elegant dwellings and gardens on every block in the city. When James continued to talk with the man seated to his left, Patty, a real estate saleswoman, demonstrated that she'd been listening at style one empathic level. She explained to me that

Seattle was America's first planned city. After the all-consuming 1910 fire, the Seattle City Council drafted stringent regulations for external features of any new building. City regulations allowed zero deviations. Every detail was planned, from similarly designed attractive window frames to neatly cut grass at the sidewalk. By explaining Seattle's exquisite postfire rebuilding plan, Patty showed that she'd realized my intention and personally related to the topic.

Style two, "hearing words but not really listening," is the most difficult style to detect. The speaker may be deceived into thinking that his concepts are being grasped by the listener.

C) Shifting Back and Forth

Burley-Allen's third style of listening, "shifting back and forth" (i.e., "listening in spurts" or "tuning in and tuning out)" also lacks empathy. Like Burley-Allen's style two, style three is emotionally distant. Because the listener is prepping his own refutations while pretending to listen, his awareness turns off and on like a light switch in the hands of a one-year-old.

A couple of years ago, I went south into style three until Sophie told me, "Bill, you listen, and then you don't listen. It's annoying!" Well, she was correct. It took me a couple of months of self-observation to erase my disconnection. If you observe your inattention or are caught out by your partner, tell her something like, "Sorry, it's true. I'm not fully listening to you." Such candor generates more harmony.

Trait Three of Investigative Dialogue: Inquiry into **Why?**

A discussion of inquiry into *why* could become a whole book. Readers could easily add more tactics to the two I describe below.

First, we can *rephrase a comment and change it into a question that prompts a deeper answer.* Second, we can *ask more detailed questions.*

An example of *rephrasing* is, "You say you like your job, so what's the reason why you want to retire?" Now we're moving into the *why* or motivation area. Perhaps this *why* is fear of social and emotional isolation if he quits work. Maybe the *why* is a potential and troubling diminished income. Who knows until we hear a reply to our inquiry?

As another example of rephrasing, the inquirer can ask, "You say, 'I love karate.' Great! So with this pleasure with karate, why is it hard for you to practice twenty minutes each day?" Perhaps the subject's simple answer is that practice is boring. Perhaps the speaker's more basic and lifetime negative belief is, *I can't really ever be a good fighter.*

Inquiry method two is *to ask more detailed questions.* A board member can state to a friend, "I'm afraid to speak up at our meetings." The listening partner asks, "Would you still have fear if you figured out the two most pressing concerns facing the board? And then researched the solutions before your next meeting?"

Now the fearful board member can ask himself, *Would my fear go away if I researched the two top concerns?* If his intuitive answer is yes, his fear is largely dissolved.

The crafty, subtle negative beliefs that we have about ourselves and others must *be uncovered* if we desire to live more happily. Anyone committed to investigative dialogue can gently elbow another person into increased clarity about negative beliefs. Investigative dialogue is a device to crack open subconscious ignorance.

At a party I sat next to a friend I'll call Geraldine. Our conversation was so interesting that I wrote it down when I got home. We both personally related to her topic: *How does a therapist provide maximum benefit to a client who wants only empathy and not inquiry.* Even with people dancing in front of us to low volume Beatles music, we dialogued about this topic for at least an hour.

I asked Geraldine, "How are things going?"

"I'm totally *exhausted* with a client!" Her tone and facial expression displayed her distress as she spoke about twelve sessions of tedious listening. Geraldine said, "I'm not sure I want to keep being a therapist. Thirty years is enough!"

I paused for a moment before asking, "Do your other clients tire you out like this one does?"

"No. I still like working with them."

"Would you consider keeping your practice if this tough one left?"

Geraldine went silent for at least a minute, and then said, "Probably." She nodded to confirm her choice. I thought, *Geraldine is too attached to this client.*

"Tell me a bit about this client."

She paused again and nodded. "She's middle-aged and wants empathy. I listen to her talk about the reasons she loves her boyfriend and the reasons why she wants to leave him. During our twelve sessions, she rehashes the same old stories. I can't give her empathy any longer."

"Okay," I said softly while I was breathing in Geraldine's data. An epiphany expressing itself as an *ahaaaa* feeling swept up from my stomach to my shoulders.

"Geraldine, you can show her how to *inquire*. For example, you can tell her to write her thoughts and feelings in a notebook."

"I did that. She won't do it."

"Oh? Why not?"

"She doesn't want to."

"So . . . can you ask her to write out her *reasons* for not wanting to describe her own emotions?"

Geraldine stared straight ahead for a minute before replying, "I never thought of that." She extracted a pen from her purse and wrote out two sentences in a small notebook.

"Something else, Geraldine."

"Yes?" She was 100 percent attentive.

"You've been focusing on *empathy* for this client. Doesn't she need to learn how to *inquire* into her thoughts and feelings?"

Her face was expressionless for a while until she frowned and answered, "Yes . . . Yes." Again Geraldine doodled words into her notebook.

When she'd completed her writing, I asked, "Is your empathy for her a substitute for her lack of clarity about what she wants and doesn't want from a man?"

"Yes . . . actually it is." She scribbled more sentences into her notebook before saying, "Definitely!"

"And isn't clarity what delivers us from suffering? With clarity, this client can choose to stay with this man for a short time, a long time, or forever. With clarity, she won't take on responsibility for his attitudes, yet will keep telling him what she wants. How he responds to her requests will teach her if she really wants to remain with him or not. So, again, doesn't your client require clarity first?"

Geraldine shook her head with wonderment. "Definitely." She grimaced. "She might not want to talk about this."

"So . . . what do you ask next?"

A full minute passed before Geraldine laughed and answered, "I ask her, 'Why don't you want to talk about what brings you here?'"

I laughed with her. "Exactly. Inquiry is critical. But that doesn't mean that you can't be empathetic. You just don't get stuck in it."

More note-taking before Geraldine asked me, "Anything else?"

I paused for a while. "Maybe one more thing. You don't normally get trapped like this with clients. But it happened in this case. Outside of her craving for empathy from you, is there anything else that might have gotten you emotionally attached to being empathic all the time with her?"

She glanced upward at the ceiling, then downward while contracting her shoulders back and then forward. She stared at me as if I was her executioner. Then she smiled.

"Yes . . . I'm close to the same issue with a new man I'm sort of dating. I want him . . . but I don't like some things about him." She wrote a sentence or two.

"So . . . are you trying to gain clarity with *yourself* about your man? Are you restricting your own inquiry by needing to have continuous empathy with a client tortured by the same issue?"

The host passed by and offered us a bowl with huge cookies in it. He said, "You're talking nonstop. Is it about the Beatles?"

Geraldine grinned. "About how they brought Hinduism to the West?"

"Great!" Our host put a cookie on Geraldine's plate and stepped to his left to offer them to two women seated there.

Geraldine ate the cookie. She declared, "Right on. I continue to be empathic with her, but I'm not clear about my own ambiguity with my man."

She finished our dialogue by telling me that she'd type her notes, study them, and use a new approach with her client when they met the following week. She said, "I'll tell you how it goes the next time we meet."

Two weeks later, during our coffee break after the Sunday sermon, Geraldine sat down next to me. She said, "It came out well. I politely kept asking her to inquire. I didn't just sit still and listen to her. She finally began to ask herself questions about why she's so passive in this relationship. Maybe twelve sessions of just listening to her were necessary for her to finally start self-probing. In the future, I'll have a different mix of listening and inquiring with clients like her. And I'll be freer in my relationship with my boyfriend."

"Like telling him what you want and don't want?"

"Right."

"Sounds good. As we were analyzing your relationship with this client, I was taking a peek at the up-down relationships I've had with woman."

Meditation on Investigative Dialogue

Master the following three questions so that you can employ them during a dialogue that can create a "why?" or "opening up" question. Perhaps you're dialoguing with a colleague at lunch, with a friend meeting for a heart-to-heart talk, or with a stranger at a party.

1. Am I relating to the subject?
2. Am I listening and speaking empathetically?
3. Am I inquiring with friendly-sounding questions prompting my partner to go deeper?

You can, after a conversation and when you're alone, write down answers to the above questions. Keep three-by-five-inch cards in a shirt pocket with RLI scribbled on each card. At least once a day, write out your R-L-I realities on a card and review any notes that night.

An example of note card entrees follows.

Relate to topic	Listening	Inquiry
Yes, money abuse by a family member grabbed me.	Okay until he took too long getting back to money abuse. Bad listening then. Then okay until finish.	Took my time letting him reveal facts. My questions penetrated. Soft tone helpful when his tension came in.

After following this procedure with acquaintances and friends for a week, write out your conclusions in your notebook. Has this procedure worked? How well? What changes need to be made?

A Sufi approach to empathic listening is the in and out breathing of chapter 4's meditations on consciousness. The adaptation for investigative dialogue is below.

We breathe in whatever is said by our partner as we move into
inner silence. Then we out-breathe his or her ideas.

This breathing tool powerfully ensures our full presence in the dialogue. If you do this proposed practice in conjunction with R-L-I, you'll discover that mastery of investigative dialogue can occur within a month. It's not difficult to learn. Now, for the rest of your life, you can experience the pleasure of being a staunch friend. If your partner has a predisposition to self-investigation, she'll appreciate you nudging her toward shedding her negative beliefs.

Chapter Summary

In a truly intelligent culture, an experiential, learner-centered class about interactive investigative dialogue would be a prerequisite for marriage, having children, or any executive or teaching position.

On our growing-up journey we can usefully practice investigative dialogue. At least once a day we can apply the three major traits to resolve a speaking partner's issue. We *relate to the topic, listen empathically,* and *inquire into* why?

Listening demonstrates three distinct modes. *Empathic* listening is 100 percent presence with the speaker's intention. A paltry species of listening is *hearing words but not really listening.* A still poorer mode of listening is *listening in spurts.*

With inquiry, we ask fundamental *why* questions.

Entering one or two of your daily R–L–I (relating, listening, inquiring) responses on a three-by-five-inch card, plus writing this data into a notebook once a day, can augment your mastery of investigative dialogue.

This book's topics all intersect. The conscious awareness of chapter 1, deflowering negative beliefs with their add-ons of chapter 2, the four OFRA resolutions of chapter 3, and chapter 4's focus on silence inducing insights are all present in investigative dialogue. This book's approach to growing up and waking up is holistically integrated.

Chapter Six

RELATIONSHIPS—ANOTHER GROWING UP CHALLENGE

> Being deeply loved by someone gives you strength
> while loving someone deeply gives you courage.
> Wei Wu Wei

Romantic Love Is Not Intimacy

Of the many relationship books I've studied, the one I like best is *A General Theory of Love* by three psychiatrists, Thomas Lewis, Fari Amini, and Richard Lannon. The following passage depicts the causes of good and bad relationship.

"Because relationships are mutual, partners share a single fate: no action benefits one and harms the other. A couple shares in *one* process, *one* dance, *one* story. Whatever benefits the *one* benefits them both; whatever detracts, hurts and weakens both lives."

In our culture, romantic love erroneously refers to the "*one* process, *one* dance, *one* story." Instead, romantic love's often hidden assumption is, *We need each other.* Heavenly qualities are assigned to the beloved. The beloved complements the lover because the lover can barely survive without the saving graces of the beloved: *He dances so smoothly. She has what I lack.* The underlying belief of romantic love is, *He/she has something that I don't have but need.*

What is the logic of these beliefs? If this emotional deficit didn't exist, no two people would ever get together. Wrong! This species of complementary neediness is *not* "A couple shares in *one* process, *one* dance, *one* story." Instead, romantic neediness is "whatever detracts, hurts and weakens both lives." Writer Oscar Wilde pointed out this truth: "The very essence of romance is uncertainty."

This truth might dismay filmmakers, TV advertisers, teen daters, and romantically fixated men and women. This addictive "lack of" brand of neediness ensures that romantic love will become a substitute for true *oneness*, authentic caring, solid intention to live together in harmony, and the requirement that both partners consciously evolve out of their own emotional attachments. Practically all of us have experienced romantic love followed by disappointment and regret. All in all, our culture does not provide a realistic love relationship model.

The romantic lover views the beloved as an *object*. The lover becomes fascinated with the beloved's voice, language, hair, attitudes—everything. The beloved becomes a dream come true: *What I've always longed for.* Lovers dance together in a spell, hypnotized, their serotonin levels skyrocketing as if they had overdosed on Ecstacy. This seventh heaven can last for months or even years if the couple keeps dating. What happens if they live together or marry? After one to four years, the great majority of relationships become bumpy and confrontational. In most cases, the romance degenerates into moodiness, irritation, anger, or desire to be alone.

Like romance, children can temporarily strengthen a relationship. One strong suit is, *Our children are making our marriage better.* Our affection for our children enhances fondness for our mate. Yet, as a strong suit, it also can set us up for the fiction that our relationship requires children. I'm not saying that children aren't marvelous to have around. They can be a superpositive aspect of a solid relationship. Yet any *reliance* on their company can lead to parental stress. Certainly, children don't deserve to be considered the bad wiring that careens the plane into the ocean.

Young children are lively, spontaneous, and responsive to everything. To some degree, children are the real *us*, the *What I am* without our emotional add-ons. We can desire to be as lively as they are.

When kids reach adulthood and are ready to leave, our parenting becomes less crucial. With children out of the house, many parents yearn for their former affectionate contact with them. If a couple significantly misses their recently departed children, that's a flashing red sign that the relationship is bumping over a decrepit, rutty road. An empty-nest syndrome might actually be an empty-relationship syndrome. Mates must build real intimacy or fall into lethargy.

Yet we can hazily think, *I have a good marriage. The kids are getting educated. We own a nice house. We have friends we see every week. No one's been unfaithful. Our marriage is okay.* Yes, that might seem true, but a close analysis would reveal that "okay" means D+ to C-, a barely passing grade, just enough to stay in class. However, if vigorously inquired into, this species of relationship produces the answer *no* to these questions:

Have you realized your purpose for this partnership?
Are you living fully and completely with present-
time experiences?

> Can you genuinely answer the questions Who am
> I? and What am I?
> Are you really enjoying your mate most of the time
> you're together?

In sum, even though our culture doesn't assist us in asking these questions, they're always boiling in our subconscious precortex and limbic brain.

Chapters 1 to 3 detail the childhood conditioning pushing us to grow up. These same beliefs also foster romantic love and can jar us into further growing up in our relationship. We can begin with romantic love, fall into tedium or antagonism, commence growing a better relationship, and finally inch into a truly enjoyable, harmonious, affinity-based partnership casting out personal neediness.

Romantic love and its eventual conflict are a species of belief-based conditioning. The ups and downs of refining a relationship are integral to the growing-up phase of the spiritual path. Authentic intimacy equates to enlightenment. I intuit that crafting a secure, joyous, intimate relationship is close to spiritual awakening. The necessity of undermining negative beliefs is identical. The same independence-interdependence fusion exists with happy mates and within awakened individuals. Until modern times, Sufi meditation masters wouldn't take students who didn't live with a partner. They wanted their students to live in more stressful circumstances in order that their conditioned add-ons could be readily inspected.

Likewise, people who practice tools like OFRA and investigative dialogue are helping out their mates. "Whatever improves the *one* benefits both."

We certainly improve ourselves when we increasingly love ourselves. The following meditation is a tool for that objective.

Loving-Kindness Meditation

If an intrusive thought attacks your meditation, breathe it in on an in-breath and release it on the out-breath with a grateful thought such as, *Thank you, intruding thought, for giving me the opportunity to release you.*

Spend three to five minutes for each of the seven objects of meditation.

Consciously breathe in and out a few times to relax.

Bring into mind *someone whom you love.* Breathe into your heart his or her image and your love for that person. Breathe out this image and love into the vastness of all space.

Bring into mind a *family member* whom you love. Breathe into your heart his or her image and your love for that person. Breathe out this image and love into the vastness of all space.

Bring into mind a *friend* whom you love. Breathe into your heart his or her image and your love for this friend. Breathe out this image and love into the vastness of all space.

Bring into mind a *neutrally attractive person* whom you would like to love. Breathe into your heart his or her image and your greatest attraction to that person. Breathe out this image and attraction into the vastness of all space.

Bring into mind *someone whom you dislike*. Select a single trait you do like about this person. Breathe into your heart that single trait. Breathe out into the vastness of all space your respect for this trait.

Bring into mind all the *live creatures* of the universe whom you love. Breathe into your heart their images and your love for these creatures. Breathe out these images and love into the vastness of all space.

Bring yourself into mind. Breathe into your heart your image and your love for yourself. Breathe out this image and love into the vastness of all space.

Mindfulness Births Independence and Harmony

Researchers have found that the most difficult relationships are male-female partnerships—more difficult than parent-child, boss-subordinate, teacher-student, even author-publisher.

Robert, in his eighties, and Angela, sixty-five, have been married for twenty years. Both are faithful, highly educated, resourceful, and excellent in their former careers—Robert as a university professor of mathematics and Angela as a middle-school counselor.

Regarding their situation, I observe that tangled knots in life-partnership relationships are attributable to beliefs existing since childhood. The person tied up with add-ons is not mindful and hence emotionally distant from his mate. Robert informed me that his father had harangued him with, "You've got to study and work hard. And never let anyone handle your money. Watch out for American women. They don't let the husband run the business."

At thirteen Robert used his bicycle to distribute morning newspapers and continued to maintain himself by working part time in clothing shops until he finished his bachelor's degree in mathematics at the University of California in San Francisco. He had scholarships that financially guided him to his doctorate at Stanford University.

From day one in his infancy, Robert was trained to be successful. His parents escaped from Germany before Hitler commenced his mass annihilations. Their mantra was "education, education, education." Also, "Be the smartest man in the world in a science field."

The childhood training of Robert was a strong suit, enhancing his life and also limiting it. Robert's strong suit is *dedication to learning and working hard to earn money, plus vigilance about keeping control of my money.* Robert's dazzling intellectual capacity was initiated by his parents. Once they removed themselves from Germany, Robert could make a name for himself with *education, education, education.* Robert had to be the best informed man in existence, and he demonstrates that childhood belief whenever he talks about anything from the top possible speed of a baseball pitch to the likelihood we'll ever meet up with humans from another planet.

These attitudes lifted Robert to university status. It also soured his relationship with Angela. He couldn't envision her as a true partner, an equal in conversations, in financial planning, or in management. She became tired of his controlling monologues and money hoarding.

I've spoken with Robert maybe twenty times. Not once has he varied from his type three listening in spurts. I've spoken about my love of table-tennis, my diabetes, and Emily Dickenson's soul-shaking poetry, but Robert insists on converting the topic into something else. He responded to my comment about the beauty of a Venice Beach, California, sunset with, "Nothing approaches a star cluster seen through a spaceship window."

When Angela hears Robert conversing with anyone, she shakes her head as if witnessing an approaching tornado. She told me, "I can't discuss anything with him. By my third sentence, he's got a lecture going."

I asked, "Is that the way he taught, or did he have a back-and-forth with his students?"

She laughed while blinking for emphasis. "He stood in front of the blackboard and talked to it while drawing equations. The students didn't even hear or understand most of what he said."

"Why didn't they fire him?"

"Because he was famous around the math world. He published in major scientific journals. He traveled everywhere for conferences."

"Why don't *you* fire him?"

"Because he has a good heart in other ways. I'm free to do what I want with my time. And he's too old for me to leave him."

Angela has considerable independence and mindfulness. Robert has some independence and little mindfulness. Robert lacks all three ID qualities when Angela speaks: personally relating to the topic, empathetic listening, and inquiry into *why?* His mandate is, "Just listen to *me!*"

Angela profoundly exhibits all three traits. I treasure our conversations, and she has a trainload of friends. She's the chairperson for her local political party meetings.

How do we pass beyond the childhood beliefs that cause Robert to fracture his relationship with his wife? How do we dive into romantic affairs without emotionally drowning? How do we love our children without using them as a pseudo-remedy for lackluster relationships? Chapters 1 to 5 cite resolutions such as the two journeys of growing up and waking up, the OFRA approach, several meditations, and investigative dialogue. The most nitty-gritty answer, at least for me, is the *conscious awareness* or *mindfulness* that chapter 4 lays out as *presence,* an inclusive *here-and-nowness.* It liberates us from ol' ego's barricade against creative thinking. Mindfulness propagates a multilayered emotional harmony indispensable for an intimate, joyous relationship. *I need him to be happy* must vanish. *I love to be around her* must flourish. That's unity. Unity is one half of the pie.

The other half of the pie, *independence,* is characterized by terms such as *personal power, self-confidence, soul,* and *I am-ness.* My dictionary defines "independence" as "not determined or influenced by someone else."

We must be mindfully independent to be happily unified with our partner. Yet independence is often misinterpreted as the arrogant, judgmental ego or lower self. I say, "No!" Authentic independence is *intelligently taking care of ourselves.* If we don't pull out this piece of the pie from the frig and eat it, we're incomplete and dissatisfied. Loving ourselves is crucial. In this context, Angela must master a radical independence of any neediness to have a good conversation with Robert. Such neediness is like asking a cat to recite poetry. She must properly, smoothly contradict Robert's narcissism.

I say "Yes!" to the superb phrase from *A General Theory of Love,* which I'll repeat: "Whatever improves the *one* benefits both; whatever detracts, hurts and weakens both lives." This *one* process means giving up our ego while cementing in our emotional independence.

Sophie is independently mindful. In OFRA fashion, she fully observes, feels, takes responsibility for, and takes action about my torn T-shirts and spikey hairstyle. At the same time, her clarity and heartiness are independent of my wishes. She wants what she wants, and what she wants does benefit me: "Whatever improves the *one* benefits both." I accede to her desires because I'm mindful that her aesthetic sensibility is often richer than mine.

At least once a month, Sophie craves Sierra Club hikes. Nine years ago we accidentally met in a cave at Catalina Island off the coast of Southern California. I was exhausted from hiking and slipped into a cave to lie down. Sophie was there and invited me in. I do enjoy these hikes but don't have her passion for hiking in nature. Just sitting and watching nature is fine for me. Yet I plan at least one hike a month. Also, I scout out a two-to three-week trip for us during her summer vacation. This summer we'll drive from Los Angeles to the Abbey Bach Festival in St. Benedict, Oregon. Sophie's passion for traveling has crept into my arteries. I now look forward to our trips and hiking escapades. Carrying out Sophie's wishes has brought us unity and, gradually, has furthered my pleasure with hiking and trips.

Sophie implored me to be mindful about her feelings, including negative ones. She urged me to pipe down my analyses of her psyche's needs and listen 100 percent when she's upset. Now I do so with greater empathy—and have gained greater independence from any need to take responsibility for or to fix her emotional attachments.

I finally apprehend that she's a "body person" whose emotionality flows out with *whatever* her body is experiencing. When she comes home tense from a thorny day with still maturing high school kids, she's withdrawn. She wants to watch TV movies, eat, and sleep, "none of which serves me well," she admits. Her edginess, if unrelieved, stretches into the weekend.

Once I apprehended her behavior, we united OFRA responsibility and action. She agreed to arrive home by 4:00 p.m., rather than dally at school or shopping. If she wishes, she sleeps for an hour. Then we exercise at the gym, swim, walk, or attend a yoga class. We do a meditation at least three or four times each week after dinner. This program substantially eliminates her tenseness after work. Our evenings and weekends have become much more energetic and congenial.

Sophie also gives me what I desire. Giving = unity, and intelligent desiring (not needing) = independence.

Because I like to club dance at least once a week, I wanted to practice ten minutes each evening so that we'd achieve better muscle memory and thus more flexibility of movement around the floor. She agreed to devote at least ten minutes each evening to practicing steps, not dancing to music, which she prefers. She has done so.

Another of my needs is to be on time for meetings. Sophie is fine with being late, a habit that frustrated me. I once threatened to leave without her if she was late styling her hair and putting on fashionable clothes. She's stopped her tardiness. Now, we walk to the car with adequate time allowing for slowdowns due to heavy traffic.

I asked Sophie to assist me with a complex diet that took three months to finish. She did, and now buys and cooks exactly what I need.

I wanted a partner who could assess my social world with wisdom, so I asked for more of her knife-edge analysis of people and groups. An example was our dialogues about my disastrous meetings with a church committee. Since our church loses members as often as it gains them, I desired to grow our church with more advanced, learner-friendly, experiential instruction in adult classes. The committee was focused entirely on logistics and cognitive instruction for new class teachers (i.e., intellect over participation). My unrealistic expectation that they would incorporate mindfulness into classes made me lash out harshly at them for their refusal to even consider this possibility. Assisted by Sophie's investigative dialogue, I realized that I'd been naïve about committee members' capacity to understand any advanced species of instruction.

One member asked me, "Why do you push mindfulness at us? You teach the meditation class, so that takes care of this mindfulness business for this church." If I had *fully* listened to this sentence, it would have shaken me out of my ignorance about the committee's predisposition.

My painful two-month confusion about this issue, my meditations, and my dialogues with Sophie ended my naiveté about anyone. This emotional catastrophe was the most illuminating, most freeing event of my life. From start to finish, Sophie employed investigative dialogue with me.

When my gullibility vanished, I became more successful in promoting mindfulness at my church. Interestingly, the three committee members who had disparaged me all took a mindfulness seminar six months later. I sat across from them and observed their enjoyment of the seminar. Since then, they've been very friendly with me. Maybe a verbal blastoff occasionally promotes good changes.

What worked for me can pass muster for you. We must cultivate our independence, and, therefore, *We must persist with appropriate requests for what we want,* even if it takes a long time to get it. If our partner eventually responds to a request, and we likewise respond to his or her request, we become intimate. That's the route out of the hurricane energies of a relationship. For relationships to function at a high level, they require two *independent* souls peacefully bundling together as *one* unity.

The prerequisite for such independent yet harmonious interdependence is mindfulness. Sophie had to become more mindful of the fact that she had nothing to do with the abysmal attitudes that many of her students brought to class. I had to become aware that church committee members were fixated on logistics and, therefore, were unable to consider mindfulness a holistic goal for everything the church does, including how committee meetings are run.

Meditation on Dimensions in Relationships

The thesis of this Buddhist meditation is that when we love ourselves we spread love to others.

Sitting with a straight back and shoulders back posture is correct for this meditation. You can either say or think the italicized sentences for each stage. Slowly inhale the first sentence and exhale the second sentence. Next, spend three to five minutes in silence for each stage. Consciously experience your in-and-out breathing in order to lessen any intrusive random thoughts.

Stage one

Inhale: *I am loved by the heart.*
Exhale: *I love the heart.*
Silence.

Stage two

Inhale: *I am in love with love.*
Exhale: *Love overwhelms me.*
Silence.

Stage three

Inhale: *I am all beauty.*
Exhale: *I am all love and joy.*
Silence.

Stage four

Inhale: *I am a conduit for the heart to reach all things.*
Exhale: *All beings are a part of me.*
Silence.

Stage five

Inhale: *I am the source of love.*
Exhale: *Love is within me.*
Silence.

Chapter Summary

This chapter's meditation is powerful if practiced regularly. It can move us toward self-love, the prime prerequisite for loving others.

Our culture has instilled romantic love as the sine quo non of good relationships. Sorry, but that belief doesn't work. Romantic lovers crave for their partners to load them up with self-love, confidence, and joy. That might work to some extent while they date or live together for one to four years, but then it usually vanishes. Negative beliefs from childhood are triggered and take over. Acceptance and harmony dissipate. Couples must deeply understand that living together or marriage is a challenge for each to *evolve into greater independence* and *into greater appreciation for their interdependence*. As *A General Theory of Love* states, "A couple shares *one* process, *one* dance, *one* story. Whatever improves the *one* benefits both; whatever detracts, hurts and weakens both."

I'll repeat this chapter's base mantra: mindfulness births intimate unity and independence. That's the reality of an advanced relationship. Unity-independence requires judiciously applying the three traits of investigative dialogue. Partners who master investigative dialogue can guide themselves through a dilemma much more thoroughly than a therapist can. A therapist is onboard our ship one hour each week, while a partner is on deck 24/7. A mindful mate can assist our navigation through tempestuous emotional waters.

We can recognize that we are evolved in certain areas and weak in others, and regard the relationship as a pathway toward self-evolution. We might write a better habit on the refrigerator and practice it for a month. I wrote and practiced "classier dressing for a month," while Sophie wrote and practiced "on time for any activity." It worked!

Chapter Seven

THE ULTIMATE CHALLENGE—
OUR CULTURE

> If you keep a green bough in your heart,
> a singing bird will come.
> Buddhist proverb

America's Stressful Culture

"You're writing a chapter about *culture*?" a friend asked. "That's too huge a topic for a book like yours. Six libraries won't begin to describe any culture."

I'll do my best. We're vulnerable to our culture. Its values have been implanted in our psyches and leaked into our behaviors, just as coughing emerges from a cold. How do we deal with this culture?

This book's answer is meditations that stress OFRA, observe, feel, responsibility, action. Each of us is responsible for our observations of cultural traits that grind us down. Each of us must feel this grinding, take responsibility for a healthy response to it, and apply actions to release the stress and rediscover our own happiness and life purpose.

"Culture," according to my American Heritage Dictionary, is "The totality of socially transmitted behavior, arts, beliefs, institutions, and all other products of human work and thought . . . these products considered with respect to a particular category, such as a field, subject, or mode of expression: *corporate culture.*"

The key term in this definition is "beliefs." Behaviors, arts, and institutions arise from specific beliefs. Monotheism, a belief in a single, all-powerful deity, is a widespread religious conviction in our culture. Sixty-five percent of American adults hold to this belief. Americans generally have faith in monogamy and also accept divorce if they consider it necessary.

For decades, America has been famous as "the place to go." One greatness of the United States was its accommodating immigration policy. Another greatness has been its pliable capitalism, enabling upward shifts from poor to middle class to rich for those willing to work hard and/or become more educated. Our natural resources are immense. Freedom of religion built upon the separation of state from religion has guarded the American dream. The Founding Fathers with their Constitution and Bill of Rights set us up for more worthwhile lifetime choices. The *independence* discussed in chapter 6 has been America's strong suit.

The last forty years have witnessed a downturn in this success story. You might disagree with the following descriptions of American culture, but they reflect statistics and concise commentary by scholars. Americans work longer hours than people in any other industrialized society. American employment is generally stressful. No six-weeks-a-year vacation as in France. No two-hour lunch break with family as in Mexico. No gyms to work out as provided by many Japanese companies. To oppose employment pressure, working at home has become increasingly common.

To realistically approach our hard-working American culture, I'll first describe details of employment at a high school in Los Angeles. Although many superb middle and high schools exist, national student performance statistics reinforce my descriptions of Los Angeles as representative of American schools. The following education section takes a data-driven look at the eat-'em-up stress that middle and high school teachers suffer. If you're not familiar with this specific work environment, learn the facts. What goes on there also permeates our corporate, media, and political worlds.

The upcoming review of American education and employment isn't jolly. Nevertheless, for some readers it might provide an intellectual jump start in assessing their school and job environments. The following Meditation on Contemplative Metaphrases, especially steps 2, 3, and 4, is efficient in reducing stress occurring in these settings.

Meditation on Contemplative Metaphrases

As a sit-down meditation, take at least four minutes for each metaphrase. Before you begin this meditation, study the examples for each metaphrase so that you have a good idea how it differs from the other three. As a real-time meditation, this is a *constant*. You can perform it at any time with any uncomfortable feeling.

As you begin with each one, say it or think it, and then *rest in the silence of fortitude and compassion for yourself.*

If an add-on sneaks in, repeat the metaphrase and re-enter the silence.

1. ***May I accept my imperfections.*** An imperfection is something that you either can't change or can change only a little. It's probably with you for this lifetime.
   - A physical imperfection such as a short leg or middle-aged baldness.
   - A tendency to be uncomfortable with cold weather or with loud noises.
   - A fear of sailing on the ocean.

2. ***May I be patient with my weaknesses.*** A weakness is a trait that you would prefer not to have but might be able to change. You don't like it, and it especially is bothersome in relationships.
   - A habit of speaking your mind to someone you know well, but without listening to the other person (i.e., controlling or lecturing speech).
   - Persistent insomnia. This trait can be changed, but it requires steady application of remedial tactics.
   - Overwork at the office. The boss needs work done, and you always comply.

3. ***May I have courage to respond constructively.*** This is the classical issue with our negative reactions. We have a negative reaction rather than a positive response:
   - Not asking for what you want.
   - Not saying no to what you don't want.
   - Not carrying out your artistic, business, or lifestyle visions.

4. ***May I always be at ease.*** This metaphrase will serve you when life gets rough.
   - Your job no longer fulfills your needs. You're unhappy with it. Therefore, you can practice

inhaling and exhaling, *May I always be at ease* while you're taking practical actions to locate a new job or improve the conditions of your current one.

- You recognize that you and your mate have opposite attitudes toward travel. You like to travel, and he doesn't. As you're resolving this difference, stay calm.

Education: A Microcosm of the American Macrocosm

The Third International Mathematics and Science Study (TIMSS) tested a half-million students in math and science in forty-one industrialized countries in Europe and also the United States, Canada, New Zealand, and Asia. Of the twenty-one nations tested in twelfth-grade mathematics, the United States ranked nineteenth, with only Cyprus and South Africa lower. The United States tested sixteenth in science, with only Italy, Hungary, Lithuania, Cyprus, and South Africa lower. In a speech regarding the TIMSS research study, Pascal D. Forgione, PhD, commissioner of US education statistics, stated, "Chances are, even if your school compares well in SAT scores, it will still be a lightweight on an international scale." Dr. Forgione's analysis makes two major points. First: "By the time our students are ready to leave high school—ready to enter higher education or the labor force—they are doing so badly with science they're significantly weaker than their peers in other countries." Second: "Our idea of 'advanced' is clearly below international standards."

Beliefs about education will differ according to social class, yet most Americans' core belief about education is something like, *It's important*. Does that belief translate into, *Kids must do their homework*? No! Does it mean that class sizes must be mandated at less than twenty-five? No! Does it mean that counselors must phone parents every time a student disrupts a class or send the student home with a note about why he or she has been barred from a class for a week? No! Our deeper cultural beliefs are, *Hands off the educational system,* and, *Don't bother the parents; they're doing the best they can.*

Many students think, *I don't have to work hard and learn the material. I can pass with a D or D-. Why should I stress myself to learn this stuff? Even if I fail courses here in junior high school, social promotion will get me into high school.*

Many parents believe, "It's the teachers' job to implant good motivation in my child." That belief shields them from responsibility for ensuring that their children do homework and behave well in class.

My attitude results from conversations with Sophie, who has taught chemistry and biology for twenty-eight years. Several science teachers who have read this chapter concur with her conclusions. Without doubt, many United States middle and high schools prove more advanced than what I'll describe. Yet the statistics I cite are accurate. All in all, our culture doesn't address the issue of student or parent accountability. *Independence,* yes. *Interdependence/unity/harmony,* no.

I've been invited to many teacher gatherings. Teachers there complain about huge class size and disruptive student behavior. In her 2013 classes, Sophie has forty-two, forty-four, thirty-eight, thirty-five, and thirty students in her classes, which adds up to 189 per day. One or two rowdies can cause the instructor to struggle to maintain a teachable atmosphere. Three to five disruptors produce a tense atmosphere very difficult to correct. Everyone suffers, including good students. The ruffian enjoys his onerous behavior. He gets *attention*. He's *talking*. Supposedly, he's *powerful*.

What are other beliefs diminishing our educational system? One common belief is that kids have the right to express whatever they want and whenever they want. Consequences do exist for abusive speech or "cross-talking" while a class is in progress, but very few teachers have the time and energy to follow through with phone calls every time to parents. Even after calling a parent, within three days the poor behavior returns. The student says, "Okay, I'll do my homework and take notes, not talk so much," but old habits are hard to change. The poor behavior returns and student culture wins out over educational culture.

If the teacher tells a disruptor to quiet down, he responds with a shrug or a dismissive shake of the head. When the instructor sends a rebel to the principal, the next day he returns to class and acts the same brash way. If the teacher phones a parent, the parent says something like, "I'll talk with him—tell him to pay attention." Of course, the student continues his unruly behavior, which makes class instruction difficult. Such behavior, he thinks, is his *right*, his *character*, his *identity*, his *independence*.

The belief of properly motivated students is, "I want to learn the material and get a good grade." In contrast, the belief system of poor students leads to behavior like that of shock jocks on talk radio, where they rant, seldom criticize constructively, and use the radio as a platform for outrageous remarks. Public middle school and high school classes can echo this invectiveness.

Sophie teaches three eleventh-grade classes (one honors chemistry, two regular chemistry) and two ninth-grade biology classes (one regular and one honors). From this variety of grades and levels, we can discover the facts about our public school system. Two truths reign: (1) Honors and advanced classes operate intelligently and beneficially. (2) Basic and regular classes operate poorly.

Eleventh-grade honors chemistry students attend regularly, maintain a reasonable decorum, and do the homework. They apologize for being late to class.

In the two regular eleventh-grade chemistry classes, four or five students upset classes with verbal misbehavior. According to Sophie, only 40 percent do the homework. Poor students focus on talking and joking with each other rather than learning from the teacher and sharing their knowledge. They feel a compulsion to physically and verbally play around. Even in lab experiments that are an integral part of the course, very few have the interest and aptitude to become fully involved. Their attention concentrates on socializing and impressing each other. Image overpowers substance.

In the ninth-grade honors biology class, no one disrupts the class. Almost all students do the homework and usefully share their knowledge.

In the ninth-grade regular biology class, one-fifth are ranters. Few do the homework.

The rowdy student does not demonstrate a heartfelt feeling; he's speaking from an emotion based upon a belief that he has the right to disrupt the educational process. Cheating the system is his *right*. He "needs" to have fun and question authority.

In my opinion, Forgionne's sentence, "Our idea of 'advanced' is clearly below international standards," does not relate to weak teaching but to poor student attendance, poor listening at style two's "hearing words but not really listening" and style three's "shifting back and forth," poor homework completion, and poor parental monitoring. Yet, teacher evaluation seems to be at the top of cure lists of educational reformers. *Blame teachers.* That's the easy and safe route.

This is America—two cultures at war. First, the teacher and good students are attacked by a second cultural phenomenon of talkative attention-seekers. An honors class has few intimidators, while an advanced—placement chemistry, history, English, or mathematics class (technically, a first-semester university class) stacked with Asians might exist without a single noxious student. If the class is a regular or basic science class, the percentage of disruptive students is high. One dictionary definition of "disrupt" is to "break apart."

By and large, administrators with their well-paying jobs are concerned about *not causing waves*. They smooth over conflicts and cite absurdly complicated district regulations (i.e., they craft an okay standardized approach). Their belief is, "We have to follow district rules, avoid antagonizing parents, and produce a good public opinion of the school."

In the past, schools hired a technician who fixed equipment such as projectors, computers, printers, and scanners. Long-term technicians with credentials are now given teaching positions (although they mostly prefer technical work), and teachers must repair their own equipment. Often, little money exists for new equipment or for technicians (i.e., no support system exists, no trouble-shooting).

Sophie arises at 6:00 a.m. and leaves for school at 7:30 a.m. During her fifteen minutes of "nutrition," she usually mentors students. She enjoys a free half-hour lunch period. School is over at three fifteen, but in her old routine before she taught herself to reach home by four, she often remained until four thirty or five assisting students, preparing course materials, grading tests, or attending frequent, nonconsequential meetings. When she arrived home, she gave me a kiss, spent five minutes with me, and headed to the bedroom for "an hour of recovery time." Her bye-bye remark was, "I'm too tired to do anything." From Monday through Thursday, she still averages one to two hours late at night preparing for classes or grading tests.

Sophie also orders supplies and equipment for her classes, sometimes paying for them since her allotted yearly purchasing amount is inadequate.

It all adds up to fifty grueling hours per week.

I've been to several parties and dinners where Sophie's colleagues, including art, English, and social science teachers, speak about their stressful days. She's no exception. *All* her coworkers are tense after coming home from teaching. On Friday night, many are too wrung out to attend a movie or theater. By Saturday, they're refreshed enough to do so.

Sophie was a student and then, for four years, a high school instructor in Lebanon. There, she never witnessed negligent student behavior. She reports that students are accountable for homework, respect instructors and the educational process, and earn their grades with no social promotion allowed (i.e., the teacher not failing students who earn a failing grade).

In the United States, middle and high school instructors are fearful that if they refuse to go along with the unstated, conventional amount of social promotion they'll be fired. Sophie's percentage of social promotion of regular chemistry and biology students is about 25 percent. She hates this decrease of ethics but also wishes to keep her job.

I often joke that the public school district should pay me, or anyone else who has a mate teaching full time, an upkeep gratuity. We deserve appreciation for the emotional and physical upkeep of our partners: rubbing their backs, listening and inquiring about their grueling day at work, and being as patient as possible with a corrupt system that injures their bodies, minds, and hearts. Unfortunately, with the current economic downturn, public school teachers will endure even more students per class, little or no raise in salaries, and perhaps even a dip in pension income.

A final craziness. During a week in the middle of May, a month before the semester ends in the second week of June, all teachers must stop teaching and spend a precious week giving their students California Standardized Tests (CST). Much material still has to be covered in these six weeks, as students haven't yet read the final chapters of assigned textbooks. CST time invades all subject areas. Students care nothing about preparing for these tests or doing well on them because their CST score doesn't relate to their final grade or passage upward to the next class. However, CST test scores are widely publicized, and schools and teachers are evaluated and criticized on CST results. Administrators and legislators win out.

If you're interested in these descriptions of our American school system, keep reading. If you're bored, you can skip a few pages to the Disasterous Capitalism section.

Parents vary in their beliefs, but mostly they cling to, "My son is doing the best he can. He has his own life to lead besides attending school. He'll do well in some vocational career or at college." In regular classes, 50 to 60 percent of parents are lackadaisical about their children completing homework. Once again, we observe little if any *consequences* for poor student performance—except an unforeseen, diminished future lifestyle.

Students are shuttled into an *academic box*. In order to eliminate the strangling racism of the 1960s and 1970s, legislators shut down most of the vocational curriculum. Their understanding was that minority-race students had been denied academic (university preparation) courses. That racism, well grounded in the past, has substantially been reduced. Now, many students of any race or ethnicity slotted into academic classes could benefit from a vocational program.

Any time cabinet makers, boat mechanics, electricians, or musicians want to gain reentry to the academic world, a community college will take them in. During my thirty-three years instructing at a community college, I taught many skilled vocational workers the basics of writing and literature. Almost all proved excellent students, and many went on to university and advanced degrees. At present, we must create vocational programs for students disinclined toward academic pursuits at this juncture in their lives.

Are private schools the solution to our distraught education system? No. The state of California recently released evidence that public school math and writing classes are on balance with those of privately run schools. My sense is that parents with children in honors or advanced placement classes are, generally speaking, wasting money by enrolling their children in private schools. Parents with children in basic or regular lower-level classes might consider sending them to private schools, if they acutely research the school selected and are willing to pay a semifortune. These parents also might consider ingraining strict academic accountability into their children's hearts.

In addition, private schools leach money from students and parents at an alarming rate. This is true for high schools and also for colleges. An editorial about private colleges in the August 4, 2012, issue of *The New York Times* reads, "A Senate committee released a blistering report showing that many of these schools pocket huge profits, even though most students leave without degrees." This article also cites the National Bureau of Economic Research, which found that "People who started in programs awarding an associate degree—a big slice of the student population—reaped significant economic rewards with degrees from public and nonprofit institutions. Those with degrees or certificates from for-profits did not." A final interesting statistic is that "the for-profit sector is growing rapidly and now consumes about one-fourth of all federal education loans and grants."

With its university educational opportunities, America has shined brightly. That brightness is dimming because of high tuition charges, restricted enrollment, and fewer jobs for graduates without a technical degree. Even 40 to 45 percent of engineer graduates can't find desired employment.

Who is held liable for our lousy educational results? *Teachers!* Read the newspaper or listen to TV commentators blaming instructors. Who are the real culprits? *Students. Parents. Administrators. Legislators. Our culture.* After all, if we followed a European approach, a young person who isn't emotionally constituted to be an academic student would be placed in vocational classes or simply drop out of school. California children legally must attend high school until eighteen years old or until graduation. This absurdity is legalized cultural death.

Do teachers respond with vigor to teacher-bashing? Yes! At Sophie's school, a bunch of teachers gathered to write a condemning letter about their uncooperative principal. For a year, I'd been horrified by this principal's negative reactions to teacher suggestions and complaints. Then they signed the letter and sent it to top-rank people at the school district. These administrators sent teams of four mediation experts or counselors, who interviewed the signing teachers. Their conclusion? The principal had "followed District policy." True to form, the district had hired a principal whose sole function was to cram district policies down instructors' throats. This principal reminded me of CIA-supported corrupt autocrats all over the world who are paid billions to serve up what the CIA wants—not what the impoverished citizens desperately require.

The bald truth is that the responsibility of parenting errant children and teenagers has *defaulted* onto our educational system. The teacher functions as both an instructor and an adaptive, caring, and prodding parent. Although this parenting role detracts from effective teaching, in many classes it is essential for the class to function at all.

Many people are envious of teachers gifted with two summer off-work months, three weeks at Christmas, and one week at spring break. All of this recovery time offsets burnout. I estimate that without the summer two-month break, 25 to 40 percent of teachers would quit their jobs, even if their families ate only potatoes. Without this downtime, teachers would be emotionally sapped. As it is, 30 percent of new teachers resign in the first five years.

These restorative periods mean that teachers' hours are about equal to other American employees' yearly work hours. As cited before, Americans work more hours per day than citizens of any other culture. Insurance agents, accountants, construction workers, doctors, or bus drivers work long hours, but they don't usually take materials home to labor over. Teaching is as exhausting as being on a stage from 8:00 a.m. to 4:00 p.m., the instructor energetically attempting to teach a challenging audience—her students. Then, after the curtain drops, there's still work to do.

Over the last ten years, international testing has proven Finland the best public school system in the world. Except for the international test taken at the end of high school, Finland's students aren't tested at all. They spend their time and effort mastering and applying each class's information.

If you're a public school teacher, how can you handle the stress described so far? This book's real-time meditations can mitigate teacher stress. I provide two applications from Chapter 2's meditations.

> Replacement: If a student walks in late with a "the hell with you, teacher" smile on his face, instead of thinking, *Why am I wasting my life teaching?*, the instructor can think, *A good opportunity to lay out consequences.* She smiles back at him, then smiles while nodding her head at the class to show her awareness of his destructive devaluation of class protocol. She says to him, while pointing at the back row, "No business will hire you if you maintain your poor behavior."

> Redirection: For the same scenario, the instructor thinks, *What a jerk!* Then she redirects this thought with, *He's a loser just like the rest of this class's losers. I'll make him a winner.* After he sits down, she walks closer to him, smiles radiantly, and says, "Write this down." She pauses when he digs out a pencil from his jacket. Then she speaks in a very slow voice so that he can scribble it down, "Copy the first two pages of the chapter we're working on, and write a single sentence summarizing each paragraph."

Chapter 2's third meditation about breathing also would palliate teacher stress. OFRA of chapter 3 and this chapter's Ask the Light meditations are winners against stress.

My conviction is that abused teachers, workers, or anyone else can profitably deal with abuse with OFRA. The above illustrations exemplify observation of one's emotions, feeling them deeply, taking responsibility for them, and taking action. For me, taking action when we're abused must include at least some reference to consequences. This reference might be a short, simple one about the abuse, plus an arm stretched forward to indicate *stop*. We lose our authenticity unless we concretely respond (not react) to any abuse.

Disastrous Capitalism

How does this summary of American education relate to other species of work in our culture? To find out, you can buy lunch for an insurance agent. Ask him, "What's your job *really* like?" He'll likely reaffirm high tension, long hours, hard tasks, and working mainly by himself inside a closed-off area rather than inside an enjoyable, people-friendly room. Next have dinner with a worker employed at a manufacturing facility. Have him rate the (1) stress, (2) hours, (3) degree of difficulty doing the required work, (4) proportion of isolated work versus cooperative work, and (5) job security. Now test out these same five attributes with a bus driver, full-time grocery store clerk, and newspaper staff member.

You'll probably discover that a vexing work pattern predominates with most, if not all, of your interviewees. In addition, the 2008 economic slump has left at least 20 percent in serious employment trouble (i.e., the jobless, the partially employed, the temporarily employed, and the long-term unemployed who have quit looking for work): *one out of five American workers.*

The core problem seems to be that the rich get richer, the middle class fades out, and the poor increase. When I finished my final draft for this book in September 2013, not a single, top-rank Wall Street banker had gone to jail for violating federal regulations. These perpetrators weren't held responsible for ruining the financial lives of millions of people, worldwide. Why not? We can't applaud the hundreds of billions of dollars of public handouts that Wall Street corporations received and the massive amounts that their top brass directed into their own scandalous incomes, to lobbyists, and to politicians.

Certainly, we have to be mindfully informed about something before we can employ OFRA to out-process its corrosive effects.

The financial world is coming under increased scrutiny. The April 14, 2011, issue of *The New York Times* has a long, scrupulously researched article by Gretchen Morgenson and Louise Story entitled, "A Financial Crisis with Little Guilt: After Widespread Reckless Banking, a Dearth of Prosecutions."

> For several years after the financial crisis, which was caused in large part by reckless lending and excessive risk taking by major financial institutions, no senior executives have been charged or imprisoned, and a collective government effort has not emerged. This stands in stark contrast to the failure of many savings and loan institutions in the late 1980s. In the wake of that debacle, special government task forces referred 1,100 cases to prosecutors, resulting in more than 800 bank officials going to jail.

Henry N. Pontell, a professor in the School of Social Ecology at the University of California, Irvine, remarked in this article, "If they [regulators] don't understand what we call collective embezzlement, where people are literally looting their own firms, then it's impossible to bring cases."

Another fact dug out by Morgenson and Story shocked me.

> The Office of Thrift Supervision was in a
> particularly good position to help guide possible
> prosecutions. From the summer of 2007 to the end
> of 2008, O.T.S. overseen banks with $355 billion
> in assets failed. The thrift supervisor, however, had
> not referred a single case to the Justice Department
> since 2000. The Office of the Comptroller of the
> Currency, a unit of the Treasury Department, has
> referred only three in the last decade.

This government duplicity is summed up by a statement by Pontell: "When regulators don't believe in regulation and don't get what is going on at the companies they oversee, there can be no major white-collar crime prosecutions."

Are the rich *that* influential? The Economic Policy Institute reports that from 1979 to 2007, the average tax rate for the top 1 percent of households lowered by about 20 percent. In contrast, during this same time span, the average tax rate for all Americans dropped by just 8 percent. Even wilder, during an even shorter period, 1992 to 2007, the tax rate on the four hundred top income households (at least $350,000,000 per year) dropped by a third. The tax rate for these superrich people is *less* than that of the average American household.

The easiest way to compress all the evidence is to read *The Shock Doctrine: The Rise of Disaster Capitalism*, by Naomi Klein. This book is about "people with power who are cashing in on chaos; exploiting bloodshed and catastrophe to brutally remake our world in their image."

Schools gone sour? Banks failing or becoming filthy rich due to inordinately weak government regulation? Do these cultural failures affect our health? How about *sleep* as an example?

The stress of our culture generates sleep disorders in many people. The National Institute of Neurological Disorders and Stroke (NINDS) estimates that at least forty million Americans endure one or more sleep disorders of the seventy that doctors have diagnosed.

I won't continue with such deploring statistics by citing the average life span of Americans compared to those of citizens of other modern, industrialized countries.

In this chapter, I haven't emphasized any celebrated aspects of American culture. For example, wonderful medical service brings rich foreigners here for surgery, which is often denied for those who are poor, uninsured, only partially insured, or not on Medicare. Medicare is a medical enterprise that provides superb care for seniors. I love it. So far, I'd be broke without it.

Costa Rica has basically solved these cultural issues. Sophie and I vacationed there and questioned residents about their culture, as almost all spoke good English. These were the answers: a fine school system open to everyone; universal health care; a workable system ensuring that everyone with a regular job paying even a low wage is granted ownership of a lot plus a one-room building expandable into a decent family house within five to ten years; no military at all; clean streets; no joblessness; thriving entrepreneurship; and happy, cheerful people. What's their only problem? Impoverished Nicaraguans from the north and Guatemalans from the south are besieging Costa Rica and stretching its resources. So far, Costa Rica accepts whoever arrives.

I'm not an expert about Costa Rica, but a close friend who spent thirty years doing business in Central and South

America told me that Costa Rica is "the best country south of the American border." Obviously, Costa Ricans have so far created a successful culture by eliminating or mitigating disaster capitalism.

I asked a taxi driver, "What is the central belief that Costa Ricans have about their country?" He thought about that question for a minute or two, occasionally glancing at me so that I knew he was pondering it. Finally, he said, "We have to have a good school system and government rules that make sure everyone works and pays taxes. Yes . . . good schools, good health care, and good business. Everyone shares in a good deal."

I'm glad that I wrote down his answer. I estimate that many Costa Ricans, as the opening quotation recommends, listen to the singing bough in their hearts.

How Do We Confront Disastrous Capitalism?

The foregoing commentary might seem grim to you. How can meditation alleviate this stress? The answer is, *Apply the tools.* For example, use Ask the Light meditation to dip into any cultural intrusions in your life. After two years of meditation focused at least once a week on her teaching career, Sophie achieved a much more positive attitude toward it.

First, meditation stripped away her false expectations that had carried over from her four years of teaching in Lebanon. Los Angeles isn't Beirut, Lebanon. She had to master a tough stance with rowdies that would have been totally unnecessary in Lebanon. Now, *any* misconduct results in immediate "Quiet!" or "No more, Mister!" verbal cannon balls flung at students. Occasionally, she'll deliver something like, "Do you want to ensure that you'll fail this class?" She's also written standardized letters to parents that she mails right after school. These messages designate the parents' responsibility for their children's misbehavior. Every kid who acts poorly a few times will suffer from parental anger over a formal letter enjoining them to be responsible parents.

Teachers want to be teachers, not parents to their students. Yet, somehow, they can, to some degree, train miscreants to move toward more intelligent, worthy behaviors.

A third resolution is for middle and high school teachers to band together to publicize the truth about deplorable student behavior. Teachers often do so. Recently, the *Los Angeles Times* featured a few days of articles and reader editorial comments about the failure of public schools. The articles written by its staff and supposed experts utterly failed to address the burning issues of lousy parenting, minimal consequences for negligible student homework, and disruptive classroom behavior. In the editorial columns, only a few readers stated anything about delinquent student behavior.

What about private-sector workers' difficulties? Like teachers, business employees can reduce stress by practicing the real-time meditations of this book. If a worker can grab a minute's privacy from work, he can do a replacement, redirection, breathing, or OFRA meditation. Later, at home, sit-down meditations can assist us to ask *why* we're working at a job that depletes us with daily stress, *why* we haven't uncovered a better job, and *why* we haven't strategized how to create a work environment that truly appeals to our hearts and minds. OFRA's R of *responsibility* is well positioned before the A of *action*.

Mindful employees of firms can bond in small discussion groups. The members must vow to keep discussion details within the group confines. Practical methods of improving management can be candidly discussed. Concerns about new hiring, job safety, work hours, training for computer use, evaluating workers and managers, rest time, safety, outsourcing, facts about people quitting the firm, and promotion are valid topics. More than anything else, the sheer fact of expressing one's truths to fellow workers is reason enough to create a private group. If enough members collaborate, a memo to top bosses listing poor work conditions injurious to production might nudge them into some degree of reflection and change.

Members can meet at lunch or break periods. They also can connect by Skype at agreed-upon times at night or on weekends. Modern technology enlarges our possibilities of gathering together.

Two questions that can trigger group interaction are, *What do I want?* and, *What don't I want?* Somehow, somewhere, cracks in the corporate iron wall will become visible, and this *do want* or *don't want* inquiry expands into <u>*How*</u> do we do it? In this manner, both individual and group desires can be fleshed out. Some remediation can result.

A long while back, I was a member of such a group, and our collective issue was a nasty, controlling, ambitious, and dangerous boss who had more pliable bosses higher up the ladder. Our group met a dozen times and wrote down precisely the errors that our arrogant boss had committed. I took on the task of writing out a documentary list of his errors in a numbered format until we arrived at ten concrete miscarriages. Next, our group spent a whole Saturday afternoon role-playing how to act perplexed or innocently confused during any questioning of our role in preparing this damning material. We lucked out in that one member was a part-time actor at a local theater group. He coached us to act like pretend virgins in a brothel.

Then we slipped copies of the text into the mailbox of the two bosses above the one we detested. At this point, the two upper-level bosses *had* to recognize our boss's flaws. With clearly incendiary information, they *had* to deal with the undeniable data. The end product was successful. The monster was fired. We kept our mouths shut, although the very top manager told me in a chance meeting in our restroom, "Good job, Bill. You guys and gals did a good job." I smiled and held my hands up with palms open to indicate, *I don't really know what you're talking about.* He laughed, turned his back, and walked out the door.

Meditation on Ask the Light

This is a Quaker meditation from pages 46 and 47 of *Light to Live By,* by Rex Ambler.

This meditation reveals truths about issues in our personal lives. It encourages the light (intuitive intelligence, inner silence, divinity) to deliver answers to the meditator's questions, rather than for her to rely upon her customary, often belief-driven thoughts. The objective is to grow up into more mindfulness, more independence, and more intimacy with others. While walking, we must be mindful of the obstacles underneath our feet. When treading our growing-up and waking-up paths, we can be aware of the cultural influences that we encounter every day. Critical thinking is a necessary aspect of mindfulness.

The opening quotation, "green bough in your heart," which offers us "singing birds," is an analogy for the "light" that reveals answers after we inquire into a disturbing issue.

If you're suffering from conflicts with your mate, you might practice dimensions in relationships or chapter 8's loving-kindness meditation. For a severe tension related to a cultural issue, do Ask the Light. The following are examples of questions that can be asked during this meditation:

What is my company's /school's philosophy and management style?

What's my deepest gut conviction about this business's future actions?

Is it safe to continue working here? Would they outsource my position?

What related or ancillary businesses could I investigate for possible employment, and at what level, training, and pay?

What's the latest and future technology that will influence this business?

What new technical training would be right for what I want and need?

What are my distinct skills and knowledge that would make me welcome at different work or that would serve me as an entrepreneur?

What is my purpose in life, and how does my current work aid or detract from it?

With my skills and knowledge, is travel and living abroad a worthy possibility?

What is a positive attitude toward my potential working life?

I'll select three friends who know me well and understand my situation. One by one, I'll buy them dinner and, if they agree, have them answer each of the above questions.

Ask the Light can facilitate any one of the above inquiries about your work, school, or relationship environment. If you're buying a house, increase your clarity with Ask the Light's detailed inquiry.

If an intrusive thought comes in, you can ask the question again and then once more move into the light (silence).

If you have a powerful insight, you can briefly leave the meditation to write it down. Ask the Light can work wonders with couples. When Sophie and I finish a session, we share our insights a half hour to two hours. The instructions are below.

> One: three to five minutes. Relax mind and body. Close your eyes. Feel the weight of your body on the chair and your feet solidly on the ground. Take a few deep inhalations and exhalations. Relax your mind so much that you give up talking to yourself in your head.

> Two: five to seven minutes. Let the real concerns of your life emerge. Ask yourself, *What is really going on in my life? What is happening in my relationships? In my work? In my own heart and mind? Is there anything that makes me uneasy?*

> Three: five to seven minutes. Focus on one issue that gives you a sense of unease.

> Ask yourself, *What is it about the thing that makes me feel uncomfortable?* Get a sense of this issue's impact on your life. Deep down you know what it's all about, but you usually don't allow yourself to recognize its significance. Pay attention to any word or image that resonates with you.

Four: five to seven minutes. Verbally or silently ask yourself, *Why is it like that?*

Or, *Light, show me the source of my unease.* Don't try to explain it with usual thoughts. Just wait for the light.

You might have a simple answer such as, *Because I'm afraid.* Good! Now you can ask, *Why am I afraid?* Let the full truth reveal itself, or as much truth as you are able to take in at this session.

Five: three to five minutes. Welcome the answer. It may be difficult to believe with your normal conscious mind, but if it's the truth, you will recognize it. Trust the light. The light will show you new possibilities. If an authentic answer doesn't arise, do another meditation the following day. An insightful answer will eventually reveal itself.

Chapter Summary

Ask the Light is perhaps the most popular meditation I've taught. It illuminates painful and demoralizing beliefs and resulting stresses. Its power becomes amplified if two or more people practice it together and then share their results.

America's greatness is historically undeniable, despite serious derangements such as racism, sexism, and lack of universal health care. Yet reading any newspaper, watching TV, and utilizing the Internet to gather data about our economy will teach us that the United States has gone downhill the last thirty to forty years. How do we walk this slippery slope? Mindfulness is the base answer, and mindfulness dictates inquiry, lucidity with no naiveté, and a deep caring for your own and your family's welfare. With that orientation, a person can survive, even enjoy work, and accumulate savings.

Chapter Eight

THE DANCE OF VISION—
CREATING YOUR TOOLKIT

> Fulfilling spiritual life can never come through
> imitation. It must come through our particular
> gifts and capacities as a man or woman on this
> earth. This is the pearl of great price.
>
> Jack Kornfield

A Synopsis of the Toolkit

F riends, a loving community or family, meaningful work, and good health can foster a happy life. To achieve these goals, a toolkit of meditations can be useful.

"Toolkit" doesn't mean that you do all of this book's meditations every week or month. The key to astute use of this book is *playing with* and *testing* the meditations.

You might think, *The two meditations I like are paying off. I don't want to add anything else. I'll practice another when my intuition says I can add it without strain.* Excellent thinking! As another possibility, you might dive into this chapter's Centering Prayer with, *I'll quit talking about myself in my head and just do this meditation for a month. Forget anything else.*

The correct line derives from your own creativity. Choosing what's best for you *at this time* is the supreme self-empowerment mode. Of course, we have to practice the selected meditation for a reasonable number of weeks or months for it to saturate our mind and body.

All of this book's meditations can facilitate a higher degree of internal balance, certitude, and self-respect. In addition, meditations can relate specifically to the eight topics below. Numbers after the meditation refer to their chapter location.

1. **Awareness of surroundings**: chewing 1, awareness of awareness 1, breathing through the body 8.

2. **Recognizing and experiencing our true self as consciousness/energy**: awareness of awareness 1, centering prayer 8, chewing 8, gratitude breath meditation 3, unity and oneness 4, ask the light 7, dimensions in relationships 6, real-time and sit-down meditations on consciousness 4. breathing through the body 8.

3. **Effective communication with others**: investigative dialogue 5, replacement 2, redirection 3, gratitude breath meditation 3, real-time and sit-down OFRA meditations 3, ask the light 7.

4. **Connecting body and mind, relaxing**: All twenty meditations.

5. **Identifying unhealthy and healthy emotions and converting negative reactions from childhood into positive responses**: real-time and sit-down OFRA meditations 3, investigative dialogue 5, four

contemplative paraphrases 7, replacement 2, redirection 2, ask the light 7, gratitude breath meditation 3, breathing through the body 8.

6. **Probing and revealing our deep-seated, childhood-based negative beliefs**: ask the light 7, real-time and sit-down OFRA meditations 3, replacement 2, redirection 2, gratitude breath meditation 8.

7. **Releasing anger**: meditation on anger 8, ask the light, 7.

8. **Improving relationships**: dimensions in relationships 6, loving-kindness 6, investigative dialogue 5, ask the light 7, anger 8.

Since people can remarkably differ in their responses to particular meditations, you might discover that investigative dialogue most effectively steers you through probing childhood-based beliefs, or that chapter 2's replacement meditation best edges you into consciousness–energy. As always, *whatever works* is our guiding principle. For that reason, don't fully trust my topic designations.

A meditation is a tool, not a permanent solution or lifetime practice. Do your chosen meditation(s) 100 percent until you're finished with it—and then take it up again if it calls out to you months later. My toolkit has been criticized for not focusing on just one or two meditations. Wrong! When my class participants select a meditation, they're advised to *practice it fully* until it wears thin and then to put it into a dresser drawer for possible future wearing. With clothes, we can choose what's right for us. We hang our preferred clothes in a closet where they're visible for rewearing. This flexibility applies to meditation.

Four Meditations for Your Toolkit

These four meditations emphasize both inquiry and mindfulness. They also include real-time and sit-down meditations. Any one of them can be important for the specific learning phase an individual is undergoing. I created the first and fourth meditations.

Meditation for Orthodox Believers or for Nonbelievers

If you're a Christian, Jew, or Muslim, you might wish to practice this meditation. It's based upon monotheistic belief in a transcendent, personal, and deistic deity or God. Jews can speak to Yahway, Muslims to Allah and Mohammed, and Christians to God and Jesus, or Mary. I had no preference for one of these three faiths, so I tossed a coin, and "God and Jesus" became the written example. This meditation can be called "guidance from above," the "above" term implying loving attention flowing into you by these divinities and/or sacred humans.

Nonbelievers can address spirit, love, universal force-energy, or any preferred term as their deity. This meditation equally serves both believers and nonbelievers. It is simply one that might appeal strongly to believers.

For at least fifteen to twenty-five minutes a day, sit in a private, quiet place without others present. Practice the following steps.

1. Make sure your feet are grounded on the floor and your hands lie comfortably on your lap. Your back and spine

are straight, and your chin is softly level. Your palms are up to receive the gift of profound insight. For two or three minutes, breathe spirit into your heart. Feel spirit subtly enter your body from your feet, legs, arms, chest, lower stomach—from anywhere— and settle into your heart. Retain spirit within you when you exhale. Keep *adding* more spirit with each in-breath.

2. Now bring into mind a problem or issue you have. Perhaps it's a dislike of a trait of your pastor, doubt about continuing a relationship, distress with tithing, worry about your effectiveness in evangelizing, or unease with the sinfulness of some behavior. In your mind, rename this negative issue a couple of times. For example, convert *It bothers me that Andrew isn't a Christian* to *I won't bother him with my beliefs but invite him to services and outings with Christian friends.* During this identification of a negative issue, let spirit keep flooding into your heart.

3. Ask Jesus (or Mohammed, Yahway, or Spirit), in something close to this language, *"Lord Jesus, please guide me to an answer that will resolve my problem with* [state out loud or think out the words for the negative issue identified in step 2 above].

   Now relax again into spirit's seeping and flooding into you. If any unrelated thoughts crowd your mind, gently concentrate on spirit moving through you and into your heart. If necessary, again ask, *"Lord Jesus, teach me how to resolve this issue plaguing me. I am listening for your wisdom.* Now return once again to a silent mind and the rapture of spirit lovingly invading all the cells of your body. Enjoy your sensations of spirit's movement and the empty silence deliciously void of any thoughts.

4. When the timer rings that your fifteen minutes are up (or whatever time you choose), (A) place your hands in the prayer position, (B) thank God, his son Jesus, and the infinite spirit for their caring assistance. Express your gratitude for any answer received and for the pleasure of this entire experience.

5. Think the gratitude thoughts below or create your own versions:

   I love the Oneness of God, Jesus, and Spirit.
   I am blessed by these three that are One.
   I feel this gratitude for the One that I felt during this meditation.

Meditation on Anger

This meditation was taken from Leonard Jacobson's book *Journey into Now.* I use my own language and quote him once.

All of us carry around some repressed anger. Acknowledging it is important.

Jacobson recommends that if we are holding in a lot of unexpressed anger, we do this meditation all seven days of the week for a month.

Instructions

Think of something or someone who makes you angry. Then speak out this sentence in a loud voice with no one around: "I am so angry!" You can use many different wordings for your anger, but (1) keep the anger and words flowing, and (2) if your words stop, repeat "I am so angry!" to make them splash out.

Many Japanese companies have a special room for angry employees, who put on boxing gloves and punch a bag while screaming the name of the individual or circumstance enraging them. Likewise, with anger meditation, you can beat on a pillow, kick a wall or the floor, or clinch your hands. Be sure to keep the anger alive and bursting for five minutes. You're not trying to get rid of it: *You're expressing it.* Stomp an irritating work evaluation to death. Put your own anger at yourself for a minor fender bender into the palm of your left hand, and use your right hand to smack the car dent or the entire incident into oblivion.

The net result is to feel comfortable when anger streams out of your body and psyche. At some point during your practice of consciously experiencing and expressing anger, you'll probably start laughing at it. You'll become 100 percent responsible for it. As we experience in many of our meditations, ol' ego makes us suffer guilt and shame for so-called negative feelings. To say "Yes!" to *all* feelings and thoughts means that we've pitched ol' ego into the backseat. Once he's back there, we can become his friend, welcoming his pestering once in a while. When he tries to climb into the driver's seat, we gently nudge him back to the rear seat where he can sleep for a while. We don't want to kill him, just liberate ourselves from any strong identity with him.

A Variation on Centering Prayer Meditation

Thomas Keating's Centering Prayer is a Christian meditation. I modified it here so that everyone, including

Christians, can use it. The language is mainly my own. You can access Keating's meditation by entering centering prayer into Internet Explorer Google search.

Dedicate a couple of minutes to steps one and three, and eight to ten minutes (or more) to step two.

> One: Select a sacred word or phrase, such as *om* or *Lord bless me*, as the pointer to your intention to steadily honor and embrace the silence (God, spirit, true self, consciousness, higher self, divinity that you are).

> Two: Say this spiritual word once or twice and then relax into the silence that this word represents. Permit your body-mind to *submit* and *consent* to this identity as your truth. When standard brand thoughts and emotions arise, return to your sacred word.

> Three: To complete this meditation, stay in the silence for a minute or two.

Breathing Through the Body Meditation

> This meditation can be either real-time or sit-down.

> Think these thoughts for as long as is convenient: *I am a spiritual being having a human experience living through a physical body. My spirit, my soul's energy, moves inside and around and through me. That energy flows through me as I sit, walk, exercise, stretch, or lie down.*

Feel energy-light entering the top of your head and spreading throughout your body into every cell. On the in-breath, you can focus on it coming down from your head into your pelvic area and then, on the out-breath, passing through your heart into your environment, where its healing power expands.

Or you can experience this energy-light moving down through your body and passing through a million invisible spores into a welcoming outside environment that renews its own energy with your energy-light's assistance.

Or you can look at someone and generously pass your energy-light into their energy field so that they swing and sway and dance for hours.

I hope that you enjoyed my book, that you found it useful, and that you've begun the design of your own toolkit. You'll add and subtract meditations from your toolkit. You can rephrase meditations. You can appreciate the benefits from meditating with a friend, mate, or group. After each meditation, candid sharing of feelings and insight will slowly but steadily strip away negative beliefs. At times you'll prefer to meditate by yourself. The goal? Love for yourself and others. Independence. Interdependence and harmony. Growing up and waking up. Mindfulness.